AF398338

Martin Reén

# THE BURNING LOVE OF JESUS CHRIST
# CHRIST

## Growing in Our Bridal Identity

Korrekturläsning: Marie Enoksson
Förlag: Healing Streams
Tryck: BoD – Books on Demand, Norderstedt, Tyskland
ISBN: 978-91-527-8191-3

# TABLE OF CONTENTS

# PREFACE

This is my third book on the love of God, and yet I feel like I have barely scratched the surface. His love is so vast and deep that I could write for all eternity and still not be able to express the full revelation of the love of God. This book was born out of my encounters with Jesus Christ. I started to write a book that would have been very different from this one if everything had gone according to my plans. But as I was writing a chapter on the love of Jesus my plans were ruined. I had a powerful encounter with Jesus where I saw His beauty and His burning love for me. It was the kind of passionate love that a bridegroom has for his bride. My heart was again filled with the burning love of Jesus Christ, and I was captivated by a vision of the romance between Jesus and His bride. This is how this book was born.

I am more of a teacher than a storyteller. It has always been the Bible that has been my gateway into encounters with Jesus. I love to read, pray and declare the Word of God. It is while reading the Word of God that I have had my deepest and most profound experiences with Jesus. When reading this book, you will most likely notice that, because my aim is to give a clear picture of our Bridegroom by pointing to the Scriptures. All the chapters in this book are meant to reveal an aspect of who Jesus is, His ministry, and what He accomplished for us on the cross.

The revelations of Jesus contained within this book have given me some of the most important insights in my life with God. They have changed my life in a very powerful way and I hope that they will encourage and bless you as well. Whenever we see more of the beauty of Jesus, we are being transformed into His image a little more. It is by knowing Him as the Bridegroom that we can start to live out of our bridal identity.

When we get to know the love of the Father, we are established in our identity as sons and daughters. That will provide both security and freedom to enjoy our inheritance in Christ, as well as all the blessings of heaven. The love of Jesus Christ establishes us in our identity as His bride and it fills our lives with passion and renews our first love. It is the love of Christ that raises up pioneers and ministries that break boxes and take new territory for the gospel. I'm convinced that we need to have a deeper revelation of the love of Jesus for His bride every day. This is the reason for me writing this book. My hope and prayer are that this book will inspire and encourage you to embrace an even deeper revelation of Jesus and His finished work every day of your life. As you get to know Jesus even more, your life will become an exciting adventure that will never end. There are always greater depths and higher heights of His love to explore. I hope that this book will be a source of revelation and encouragement on your journey into the depths of God's love.

Your brother in Christ,
Martin Reén

# INTRODUCTION

*"I am the Alpha and the Omega," says the Lord God, "who is and who was and who is to come, the Almighty" (Rev. 1:8 NASB).*

This is a book about the burning, passionate love of Jesus Christ. Jesus is the Alpha and Omega, as well as the center of our lives. I have tried to write about the love of Christ, by using the eternal love story of Jesus and His bride as somewhat of a main theme for this book. One of the biblical narratives that flows all the way from the garden of Eden to the book of revelation, is the romance between Jesus and His bride.

In my previous book, *Abiding in the Father's Love,* I wrote about another important biblical narrative, that of the Father and His family. These two biblical narratives complete one another.
The Father's love provides identity and sonship, while the love of Jesus Christ provides the passion and divine romance that the Bible describe as our first love (Rev. 2:4). The love of Jesus Christ establishes us in our bridal identity. We need a deep revelation of both the love of the Father and the love of Jesus Christ. This is the reason that Jesus always leads us to the Father. Jesus even speaks about Himself as being the way to the Father (Matt. 11:25-30, John 14:1-6). The Father is always magnifying and glorifying His Son. Every time that the Father speaks in the New Testament; He speaks about Jesus. Here are two examples:

*"… and behold, a voice from the heavens said, "This is My Beloved Son, with whom I am well pleased" (Matt. 3:17 NASB).*

*While he was still speaking, a bright cloud overshadowed them, and behold, a voice from the cloud said, "This is My Beloved Son, with whom I am well pleased; listen to Him!" (Matt. 17:5 NASB).*

It pleases the Father more than anything else when we turn our attention upon Jesus and pursue intimacy with Him. The Father wants us to live with a focus on Christ and Him crucified (1 Cor. 2:1-2). Throughout all the ages, the Father's longing has been to present a pure, holy and spotless bride as a gift to His Son. That longing was fulfilled on the day of Pentecost when the church was born. We are now united with Jesus, being one spirit with Him forever. This is how we can know the overwhelming beauty of the love of Jesus Christ. *"How deeply intimate and far-reaching is his love! How enduring and inclusive it is! Endless love beyond measurement that transcends our understanding—this extravagant love pours into you until you are filled to overflowing with the fullness of God" (Eph. 3:18-19 TPT).*

### Why I Wrote This Book

I have chosen to call this book *The Burning Love of Jesus Christ*. I have a very simple motivation for writing it. I long for the body of Christ to fall in love with Jesus all over again. My hope when writing this book, is to reveal a little more of the beauty of our heavenly Bridegroom and King. My conviction is that we need to rediscover how marvelous and glorious Jesus is, and to do it again and again every day, for the rest of our lives! When we receive a greater and deeper vision of Jesus Christ, we will be transformed into His image. It is by fellowshipping with Jesus that we become established in our bridal identity, which is the key for us when it comes to keeping our hearts pure.

This is the third book in a series on the love of the God and it adds to the truths laid out in the two previous books *(Abiding in the Father's love* and *Partnering with the Love of Christ)*. You don't need to read them to understand the teaching within the pages of this book, but I highly recommend that you read the other two books as well to get more revelation on the love of God.

**The Bride of Christ & the Book of Revelation**

The book of Revelation is probably the biblical book that gives the clearest revelation of Jesus and His bride. I pulled a lot of the insights presented in this book from the book of Revelation. The approach I take when it comes to understanding the book of Revelation, is that it is an unveiling of Jesus Christ and the New Covenant. *"This is the unveiling of Jesus Christ, which God gave him to share with his loving servants what must occur swiftly. He signified it by sending his angel to his loving servant John" (Rev. 1:1 TPT).* We might have differing views when it comes to eschatology, but we can probably agree that the most important function of the Bible is to reveal Jesus and His finished work on the cross. Since the book of Revelation is part of the Bible, that should apply to that book as well. As we read the book of Revelation to see Jesus unveiled, it becomes a clear and simple book, proclaiming the victory of Christ and the triumph of the Kingdom of God! We can read it in this way while still holding on to different views of the end-times. The most important thing is always to pursue a deeper revelation of Jesus Himself.

**Three Perspectives on Identity**

The Bible describes three different perspectives of identity and it helps being familiar with those when reading this book. We're going to do an in-depth study of our identity in Christ and who we are as His bride throughout this book. For this reason, I will give a brief description of these three perspectives of identity here:

1. *Satan's perspective on identity*
   Since Satan is the accuser of the brethren and a deceiver, he is using our past sins, failures and wounds to define

who we are. According to his perspective, our identity is defined by our broken and sinful past (Rev. 12:9-10).

2.  *The human perspective on identity*
    Human beings perceive one another after the flesh (2 Cor. 5:16). This means that when people look at who we are; they define us according to our present reality. They will look at our present circumstances to figure out who we are. They use our career, education or social status, to evaluate us. In other words, people use what they can perceive about us in the natural realm to define who we are. According to the human perspective, identity is defined by our present circumstances.

3.  *The Father's perspective on identity*
    When the Father looks at us, He sees us in Christ, which means that He sees who we are about to become (2 Cor. 5:17). We are His children and He sees us as complete in Christ. According to His perspective, we are defined by who we are in Christ, and who we are about to become by the transforming work of the Holy Spirit.

It is, of course, the Father's perspective that is the only true and valid one. This is the perspective that I want to present in this book. Both the human perspective and the satanic perspective is built on a lie and both limit our relationship with Jesus. It is when the believer accepts either one or both, that they stay in bondage and are held back from living in all the blessings and benefits of the New Covenant. But the truth always sets us free, and the truth is that as Jesus is, so are we in this world (1 John 4:17). (For a deeper study on these three perspectives on identity, see chapter 5 in my book *Abiding in The Father's Love).*

## Religion and the Cold Heart

I challenge religion and legalistic teachings quite strongly within this book. There is an important reason for me doing so. The fire of God's love is an enormous threat to the kingdom of darkness, since it empowers the church to be an overcoming bride. Satan has been working non-stop since the day of Pentecost to quench the fire of God in our hearts. His strategy has proven effective, so it hasn't changed for the last two thousand years. Satan's goal is to deceive us into substituting our life in Christ for religion, and thereby creating a stronghold of cold love. Jesus addresses this when speaking to the disciples. *"And at that time many will fall away, and they will betray one another and hate one another. And many false prophets will rise up and mislead many people. And because lawlessness is increased, most people's love will become cold"* (Matt. 24:10-12 NASB). This falling away begins within our hidden life. People who are deceived by false prophets will not be recognized by their false doctrines; the sign of a deceived heart is love that has grown cold. Religion tries to quench the love of God within us by replacing a relationship of love with legalism. This is not the way we were created to live. Our Father is not religious. He wants to set us free from all religion and draw us into deeper fellowship with Jesus, setting us ablaze with His love.

## The Importance of a Revelation of Jesus

Although I am a faithful Bible reader and a lover of theology, this book is not written based on my biblical knowledge alone. I write what I have seen during my times of intimacy with Jesus Christ. We all need a deeper revelation of Jesus. Knowledge educates the mind while revelation transforms the heart. I want to pass on revelation that transforms the heart. My goal is and has always been to follow the example of the apostle Paul, who decided not to teach or know anything except Jesus Christ and Him crucified

(1 Cor. 2:1-2). Jesus is all-sufficient, and we have everything in Him.

## Each Chapter Reveal an Aspect of His Love

Each chapter within this book is written to reveal an aspect of the love of Jesus Christ. They contain some of the most important revelations of Jesus that I have received through the years and I believe that they will bless and encourage you as well. My prayer for all of us is that we may grow in our fellowship and intimacy with Jesus and that we will know Him in even deeper ways. He is glorious beyond description and He loves us more than we could ever know!

## The Activations

At the end of each chapter, you will find a section called Activations. They are there to provide practical application to the teaching. You will get the most out of this book if you take time to do these activations. They will help you to interact with the Holy Spirit to gain more revelation on the topic presented within each chapter. They are very simple to work with and they will inspire you to grow in intimacy with Jesus. All activations will involve journaling, so I suggest that you have your notebook or electronic device within reach when reading this book. In the Kingdom of God, we learn best by applying what we see. These activations will be both helpful and fun as you interact with the Holy Spirit.

# CHAPTER 1: THE BURNING LOVE OF JESUS CHRIST

There is a wildness to the love of God. He is an unpredictable, adventurous lover who always finds creative ways to express His affection for us. Zephaniah describes His loving affection toward us with these beautiful words: *"Do not fear; Zion, let not your hands be weak. The Lord your God in your midst, The Mighty One, will save; He will rejoice over you with gladness, He will quiet you with His love, He will rejoice over you with singing" (Zep. 3:16-17 NKJV)*. Most of us know that Jesus loves us, but as He expresses His love to us, He is rejoicing over us with singing and gladness. He quiets us with His love, causing us to be still and rest in His presence. The love of God transforms our hearts and renews our lives, making it impossible for us to stay the same. Jesus always shines forth through a heart that has been set ablaze by the love of the Father.

### Love Like Fire

One of the pictures that God uses to the describe His love is fire. In the Song of Solomon, we read: *"For love is as strong as death, jealousy is as severe as Sheol; Its flames are flames of fire, The flame of the Lord. Many waters cannot quench love, nor will rivers flood over it; if a man were to give all the riches of his house for love, it would be utterly despised" (Song. 8:6-7 NASB)*. His love is like a fire, whose flames can't be quenched. His love is strong enough to overcome death. The love of Jesus is so priceless that it cannot be bought. There is a holy jealousy to His love. He wants us for Himself and He longs for a bride who gives her wholehearted adoration and worship to Him. Jesus went through unspeakable suffering, even going through death itself to win our hearts. The fire of His love sets the human heart ablaze and instills it with a holy passion for the Bridegroom. As we respond to His invitation into a lifestyle of intimacy with Jesus, He will transform us into wild and radical lovers of God.

## Our God Is a Consuming Fire

*"And we have known and believed the love that God has for us. God is love, and he who abides in love abides in God, and God in him"* (1 John 4:16 NKJV). Love is not just one of God's character traits. He is love. Since Jesus is love, it is not strange that His love is described as the flame of the Lord. *"Therefore, since we receive a kingdom which cannot be shaken, let's show gratitude, by which we may offer to God an acceptable service with reverence and awe; for our God is a consuming fire"* (Hebr. 12:28-29 NASB). When the Bible speaks of God as a consuming fire, it reveals His holy passion for us. In the end, we will either be transformed by His love, or consumed by it. Jesus Christ loves us with a burning passion and He wants our wholehearted abandonment to Him. *"For the LORD thy God is a consuming fire, even a jealous God"* (Deut. 4:24). Jesus is not jealous because He is insecure, but because His love and passion for us is so pure and holy. As we surrender to Him, everything in our lives that does not look like Jesus Christ will be burnt to ashes, and our heart will be set ablaze with the fire of His love. Before Jesus returns, He will have a bride that is totally devoted to Him. This is the reason why He wants to baptize us in the Holy Spirit and fire.

## The Fire of God's Love

*When the day of Pentecost had come, they were all together in one place. And suddenly a noise like a violent rushing wind came from heaven, and it filled the whole house where they were sitting. And tongues that looked like fire appeared to them, distributing themselves, and a tongue rested on each one of them. And they were all filled with the Holy Spirit and began to speak with different tongues, as the Spirit was giving them the ability to speak out (Acts 2:1-4 NASB).*

The baptism of the Holy Spirit is an immersion in the fire of God, which is to say that when we are being filled with His presence, we are baptized in the love of the Father (Rom. 5:5). On the day of Pentecost, the disciples were overcome with the burning love of Jesus Christ and their hearts were forever transformed by that encounter. They were so intoxicated by the presence of God that they were mistaken for being drunk. Out of that encounter grew a movement of passionate lovers of Jesus that shook the Roman Empire at its foundations, causing the gospel to spread all over the world. A baptism in the burning love of Jesus Christ birthed an apostolic movement of pioneers, and it is that same love that compels pioneers and reformers to arise today. This is a wild and unpredictable fire that can't be contained or limited by religious traditions or within man-made structures. When we abide in the love of God, we will bring change and renewal wherever we go. His love will compel us to move forward into deeper intimacy and fellowship with Jesus.

### Wild Lovers of God

The fire of His love transforms us into wild believers, whose only goal is to give adoration and worship to Jesus. Moses is a great example of what it looks like to be set ablaze by the love of God. When God revealed Himself on mount Sinai, Moses immersed himself in the cloud of God's glory and walked right up to the mountain top where the fire of God was burning.

*The glory of the Lord settled on Mount Sinai, and the cloud covered it for six days; and on the seventh day He called to Moses from the midst of the cloud. And to the eyes of the sons of Israel, the appearance of the glory of the Lord was like a consuming fire on the mountain top. Then*

*Moses entered the midst of the cloud as he went up to the mountain; and Moses was on the mountain for forty days and forty nights (Deut. 24:16-18 NASB).*

When the people saw the glory of the Lord, they stayed at a distance and watched the manifestation of God's glory. Many people are still doing that today. It is easier to behold the fire of God from a distance than to jump into it and be transformed by it like Moses. I have always found Moses' relationship with God to be fascinating, because although Moses lived within the Old Covenant, he spoke with Jesus, face to face as a friend.

Moses lived a prophetic life, which gave him access to the New Covenant blessings long before they had become operational. No matter the circumstances, Moses always made the choice to draw near to God. In the same way, The Father wants us to jump into the fire of His love and be transformed by it. He wants us to be filled with holy passion, so that our goal in life is to know Jesus in deeper ways every day.

## The Atmosphere of Gloom & Doom at Mount Sinai

There is a big difference between how the fire of God manifested when the law was given at Sinai, compared to the life and power it released when the Holy Spirit came upon the church on the day of Pentecost. When Moses received the law, the atmosphere at Mount Sinai was so terrifying that the people wanted to keep God at a distance. *"For you have not come to the mountain that may be touched and that burned with fire, and to blackness and darkness and tempest, and the sound of a trumpet and the voice of words, so that those who heard it begged that the word should not be spoken to them anymore" (Hebr. 12:18-19 NKJV).* The mountain was burning with the fire of God and clouds and darkness covered the mountain.

When the trumpet sounded and the voice of God spoke, it was so terrifying that the people of Israel couldn't handle it.

They were terrified and did not want to draw near. Even Moses himself was shaken by fear: *"For they could not endure what was commanded: "And if so much as a beast touches the mountain, it shall be stoned or shot with an arrow." And so terrifying was the sight that Moses said, "I am exceedingly afraid and trembling" (Hebr. 12:20-21 NKJV).* This was not the atmosphere that would have caused the people of Israel to come closer to God. In the Old Covenant, God was hiding Himself in a cloud, while surrounding Himself with darkness. The good news is that we have a much better covenant, one that creates a very different atmosphere where the Father is revealed in glory.

**The Atmosphere of Peace, Perfection & the Presence of Jesus**

The fire of God, which appeared on the day of Pentecost brought the atmosphere of heaven. As children of God, we have not come to Mount Sinai. We have arrived at Mount Zion, the city of God. The atmosphere of this city is not filled with fear and darkness. We never have to walk through darkness and clouds to reach our heavenly Father. We live in a place where angels are ministering to us and the blood of Jesus speaks a better word, giving us open access to God all the time.

*But you have come to Mount Zion and to the city of the living God, the heavenly Jerusalem, to an innumerable company of angels, to the general assembly and church of the firstborn who are registered in heaven, to God the Judge of all, to the spirits of just men made perfect, to Jesus the Mediator of the new covenant, and to the blood of sprinkling that speaks better things than that of Abel (Hebr. 12:22-24 NKJV).*

The Holy Spirit always brings the atmosphere of mount Zion, which is saturated with the testimony of the blood of Jesus, that declares peace and forgiveness of sins. When we are baptized in fire, we become immersed in the love of Christ, which will result in transformed lives and a clearer revelation of Jesus.

### Mount Sinai - Darkness, Clouds & Fear

Throughout this book we are going to unveil the beauty of Jesus Christ, a huge part of it by looking at the types and shadows of Christ within the Old Testament. This book is called *The Burning Love of Jesus Christ,* so we are going to study the burning passion of Jesus for His bride. Because of this, it is important that we understand how the fire of God manifests in the New Covenant. We will look at that by comparing it with the manifestations surrounding the fire at Mount Sinai. When the fire appeared at mount Sinai:

- *It Brought Darkness and Clouds, Hiding God's Face (Deut. 24:18, Hebr. 12:18-19).* In the Old Covenant, the people of Israel could not have a personal relationship with God, and neither could they see His face. He always had to hide his face, relating to the people only through the priests, kings and prophets. *"He made darkness His hiding place (covering); His pavilion (canopy) around Him, the darkness of the waters, the thick clouds of the skies"* (Ps. 18:11 AMP).

- *It Caused the People to Tremble with Fear (Exod. 20:18-19).* At mount Sinai the people were shaken with fear, and even Moses was terrified. The people were so afraid that they did not want to listen anymore, even asking Moses to speak with God on their behalf since they were afraid of dying if they drew near to God (Hebr. 12:18-19).

- *Three Thousand People Died (Exod. 32:25-28).* When Moses went up to the mountain, the people pressured Aron to make a golden calf, which they worshiped as their God. This resulted in three thousand dead people. Since we are unable to fully obey the law, it will always bring death (2 Cor. 3:6).

- *It Separated the Priests and Levites from the Ordinary People (Exod. 24:1-2).* Only the high priest of Israel could enter the Holy of holies in the Old Covenant, and the priest and Levites were appointed to handle the holy things. The rest of God's people always had to relate to God through the priests and sacrifices.

**The Fire of the New Covenant Brings Life and Light**

After studying the fire of God at Mount Sinai, we will look at the day of Pentecost, which is the day that the New Covenant was established. When the Holy Spirit was poured out and tongues of fire rested upon the disciples, the results were totally opposite to what happened at Mount Sinai. As the fire of God appeared at Pentecost:

- *It Brought Light and Revelation, Unveiling who Jesus and the Father Really Is.* The Holy Spirit reveals Jesus and by beholding Him, we can know exactly who God is (John 1:18). The Father has now revealed Himself fully through Jesus Christ. *"Now the Lord is the Spirit, and where the Spirit of the Lord is, there is freedom. But we all, with unveiled faces, looking as in a mirror at the glory of the Lord, are being transformed into the same image from glory to glory, just as from the Lord, the Spirit"* (2 Cor. 3:17-18 NASB).

- ***It Caused the Love of God to Be Poured Out into the Believer's Heart, Casting Out All Fear.*** As we have seen earlier, the infilling of the Holy Spirit was a baptism of fire, where the church was immersed in the love of God (Rom. 5:5). When we are filled with the Holy Spirit, the love of the Father is poured into our heart, delivering us from fear, so that we can come boldly before the throne of grace. This causes us to minister His love to people in freedom and boldness. *"There is no fear in love; but perfect love casteth out fear: because fear hath torment. He that feareth is not made perfect in love. We love him, because he first loved us"* (1 John 4:18-19).

- ***It Caused Three Thousand People to Get Saved and Receive Life.*** When the fire of the Holy Spirit fell on the day of Pentecost three thousand people received Jesus and was born again. The fire of the New Covenant is the life-giving fire of His love. *"Then they that gladly received his word were baptized: and the same day there were added unto them about three thousand souls"* (Acts. 2:40-41).

- ***It Reveals That We Are a Royal Priesthood, and All of Us Have the Same Access to God.*** We have been made a royal priesthood and there is no longer a clergy/laity divide within the body of Christ (Eph. 2:15-18). Through Jesus Christ, all of us can come to the Father whenever we want. We have already been perfected and sanctified through the sacrifice of our High Priest, Jesus Christ. *"But ye are a chosen generation, a royal priesthood, an holy nation, a peculiar people; that ye should shew forth the praises of him who hath called you out of darkness into his marvellous light"* (1 Pet. 2:9).

The New Covenant is a better covenant built on better promises that has been secured by our everlasting Bridegroom and High Priest, Jesus Christ (Hebr. 8:6). We live in the day of salvation, and the fire of God releases life and joy from heaven. Sometimes people have made a big deal of entering the cloud and darkness to reach to God. But since God is not hiding from us anymore, the darkness and the cloud have been dispelled by the wind of the Holy Spirit. We live in the light of Christ and we can behold Him whenever we want. Since we are priests of Christ, we have been ordained by heaven to minister the new covenant in the power of the Holy Spirit. *"He has enabled us to be ministers of his new covenant. This is a covenant not of written laws, but of the Spirit. The old written covenant ends in death; but under the new covenant, the Spirit gives life"* (2 Cor. 3:6 NLT).

### Eyes Like Flames of Fire

The same fire that appeared on the day of Pentecost burns in the eyes of Jesus as He looks at His bride. *"These things saith the Son of God, who hath his eyes like unto a flame of fire, and his feet are like fine brass"* (Rev. 2:18 see also Rev. 1:14, 19:12). Jesus is gazing upon us with eyes full of life-giving love and as we are beholding His face we are renewed and filled with new life. If we focus on how to love Him more, our hearts will grow cold. But if we learn to abide in His love, our hearts will be set ablaze by the flame of the Lord. Earlier in my life with Jesus, my focus was almost entirely on what I could to for God, but I didn't know Him very well. My understanding of His love and mercy was very limited. Through the years, I have come to know Jesus and His love much better and my focus have shifted. I know that my love and faithfulness to Him will never be enough. So, I have learned to focus on His everlasting love and faithfulness to me instead. The more I see of His love, the more my heart is filled with love for Him and for other people.

## Activations

- Set apart 20-30 minutes of your day for prayer. Ask the Holy Spirit to give more revelation on the burning love of Jesus and how passionate He is for you to know Him more. Write down what He reveals to you.

- Ask the Holy Spirit to baptize you in the fire of God and to pour the love of Jesus into your heart. Invite Jesus to fill your life with His burning love and passion.

- Read the passage from Hebrews chapter twelve about Mount Sinai and mount Zion and invite the Holy Spirit to speak to you (Hebr. 12:18-24). Invite Him to give you more revelation on this passage and to fill your life with the atmosphere of Zion.

- Invite Jesus to baptize you in the Holy Spirit and fire, so that you are set ablaze with the burning love of Christ. Ask Him for an anointing to be a burning witness of His love, who spreads the fire of God's love everywhere.

# CHAPTER 2: THE LAMB OF GOD

In the book of Revelation, John was being taken into the throne room of heaven in a vision. In this vision, John sees the Father on the throne, the twenty-four elders and the four living creatures, as well as the angel armies and the heavenly beings (Rev. 4-5). But he also encounters Jesus, who appears as the Lamb of God. It is fascinating that the person with all authority in heaven and on earth is called the Lamb. Jesus is the King of kings and the Lion from the tribe of Judah (Rev. 5:5). But even when Jesus was introduced as the Lion of Judah, John sees Him as the Lamb: *"And I saw between the throne (with the four living creatures) and the elders a Lamb standing, as if slaughtered, having seven horns and seven eyes, which are the seven spirits of God sent out into all the earth" (Rev. 5:6 NASB).* Jesus is carrying the authority of a Lion, but He is meek as a Lamb, ruling with grace and self-giving love.

To know Jesus as the Lamb has been a deeply healing experience for me. The Lamb of God is gentle, full of mercy and kindness. His presence has brought much restoration and peace to my soul. We are living in a culture filled with anger and polarization, but knowing the heart of Jesus Christ has become an anchor of mercy and grace for me.

### The Anointed One Possesses All Wisdom & Power

The Lamb has seven horns and seven eyes. Horn is a symbol of God's power and authority (Ps. 89:17, 92:10). Seven is the number of divine perfection (Gen. 2:2, Ps. 12:6). This means that Jesus has all power and authority. Jesus is the King of kings. The eyes are symbols of knowledge and wisdom. This reveals that Jesus has complete knowledge and wisdom concerning all things (Prov. 15:3). He truly is a wonderful counselor (Isa. 9:6). Because Jesus has been given all authority and possesses perfect wisdom, He is called *"…Christ the power of God, and the wisdom of God" (1 Cor. 1:24).* Through Jesus Christ, we have access to the fullness of the Father's wisdom and power. The seven eyes are the seven spirits of God (Isa. 11:1-3). This is the Holy Spirit, who has been sent out all over the world. Jesus is the anointed one, filled with the Holy Spirit and power. The Holy Spirit proceeds from the Father and from Jesus Christ into all the world. *"But when the Helper comes, whom I shall send to you from the Father, the Spirit of truth who proceeds from the Father, He will testify of Me" (John 15:26 NKJV).*

Jesus did not take authority over creation by conquering the world with might. Instead, He received it by laying down His life to redeem the creation from the power of sin and death. Because Jesus was willing to do so, we can now access the fullness of His power and wisdom, which means that we have the strength and wisdom to live a life that bears fruit for God.

### The Lion That Is from The Tribe of Judah

Right before John saw this vision of Jesus, he noticed a scroll in the right hand of the Father. Unfortunately, it seemed like no one was found worthy to open the scroll. This caused John such grief that he broke down in tears (Rev. 5:1-4). One of the twenty-four elders comforted John by saying: *"Stop weeping; behold, the Lion that is from the tribe of Judah, the Root of David, has overcome so as to be able to open the scroll and its seven seals" (Rev. 5:5 NASB).*

By calling Jesus the Lion from the tribe of Judah and the Root of David, this elder shows us that Jesus did fulfill the expectation of Israel for the Messiah to be the hero that would come to deliver His people from oppression. The reason that they were confused on this matter, was that Jesus did not fulfill it the way they had expected. The people of Israel had been waiting for a hero who would defeat the Roman oppressors, but instead Jesus came as a Lamb who forgave His enemies and overcame by laying down His life. God will always fulfill His promises, but He will usually do it in unexpected ways. Jesus will always do what He said He would do, but He has no obligation to do it the way we expect it to happen.

## The Scroll with Seven Seals

The vision continues as the Lamb of God takes the scroll from the Father, while the living creatures and the elders bow in worship before Him. *"And He came and took the scroll out of the right hand of Him who sat on the throne. When He had taken the scroll, the four living creatures and the twenty-four elders fell down before the Lamb, each one holding a harp and golden bowls full of incense, which are the prayers of the saints" (Rev. 5:7-8 NASB).* It was now time for this scroll to be opened and its secret to be revealed, but no one was found worthy to open it but Jesus Himself.

It is interesting to note that Daniel had received a book with heavenly secrets, which was sealed until the time of the end. *"But thou, O Daniel, shut up the words, and seal the book, even to the time of the end: many shall run to and fro, and knowledge shall be increased" (Dan. 12:4).* We know that Daniel carried a deep revelation of Jesus Christ, but the time was not yet right for this secret to be unveiled (Dan. 7:13-14). God told Daniel to seal this revelation until the end. This end that is mentioned in the book of Daniel does not refer to the end of the world, but the end of the Old Covenant. This end came through the resurrection and ascension of Jesus when the New Covenant was put into place.

When Jesus ascended to the throne in heaven, it was time for the words within the scroll to be unsealed and the secret within it to be revealed. Only the Lamb of God was found worthy to break the seals and open the scroll to unveil its secret. The judgements that fell as each of the seals were broken, were God's judgement upon the old wineskin of religion, which marked the end of the Old Covenant and the sacrificial system (Rev. 6:1-8:5). When Jesus died on the cross, the New Covenant was fully established and the Old Covenant became obsolete. The two covenants then existed side by side for a time, but when the temple in Jerusalem was destroyed in AD 70, the Old Covenant finally disappeared (Hebr. 8:13). The New Covenant has been established and the finished work of Jesus Christ has ended the need for any other sacrifice. He is now our High Priest and King.

### The Secret Is Now Revealed

The big secret found in the scroll was the gospel of Jesus Christ, revealing *Christ in us, the hope of glory*! This secret had never been fully revealed in earlier generations. Glimpses of the gospel had been revealed through the types and shadows of the law and the prophets, but only Jesus could unveil the full revelation of the gospel. This is what the unsealing of the scroll was all about. In Colossians, Paul writes to explain how the gospel had been kept hidden and sealed for generations, but at the dawn of the New Covenant age, it was finally being fully unveiled to us.

*I have become its servant by the commission God gave me to present to you the word of God in its fullness— the mystery that has been kept hidden for ages and generations, but is now disclosed to the Lord's people. To them God has chosen to make known among the Gentiles the glorious riches of this mystery, which is Christ in you, the hope of glory (Col. 1:25-27 NIV).*

Paul addresses the unveiling of the gospel mystery in similar fashion within his letter to the Ephesians (Eph. 3:1-6). This secret had not been known to people in previous generations, but to

Paul and the believers in his generation, the glorious secret of Jesus indwelling His people had been unveiled. *"This mystery is that through the gospel the Gentiles are heirs together with Israel, members together of one body, and sharers together in the promise in Christ Jesus" (Eph. 3:6 NIV).* We have inherited all the promises of God through Jesus Christ! Jesus started to break the seals and open the scroll after He had ascended to the right hand of the Father. As that happened, judgement was executed against the old religious order so that the gospel could be preached in all the world. This is the reason that the four creatures and the twenty-four elders fell down to worship the Lamb. The scroll revealed the beauty and victory of Jesus Christ!

## The White Horse of the Gospel

As Jesus breaks the first seal, John sees a man sitting on a white horse and this man received a crown. He was then commanded to ride forth in victory:

*Then I saw when the Lamb broke one of the seven seals, and I heard one of the four living creatures saying as with a voice of thunder, "Come!" I looked, and behold, a white horse, and the one who sat on it had a bow; and a crown was given to him, and he went out conquering and to conquer (Rev. 6:1-2 NASB).*

The horse is a symbol for victory in battle or victorious triumph (Jer. 4:13, Isa. 31:1). Sometimes the horse is a symbol of ungodly strength, but this horse is white. White is the color of Christ and His righteousness, which is why we are dressed in white robes (Rev. 7:13-14, 19:14). We have been made the righteousness of God in Christ (2 Cor. 5:21). This white horse is a picture of the gospel of Jesus Christ going forth in victory all over the world. The man sitting on the horse is Jesus Himself who is sent out to enforce His victory. He carries a bow, but He has no arrows. This is because Jesus uses the gospel proclamation as the arrow that accomplishes spiritual victory and breakthrough. Here he rides alone, but later in the book of Revelation, Jesus leads an army of believers. These believers are the harvest that has been brought into the Kingdom while the gospel has gone forth in victory (Rev. 19:11-14). As the secret of *Christ in us* is being unveiled in greater depths, the gospel goes forth in triumph. The preaching of the gospel will transform the nations of this world into the Kingdom of our God. Jesus is right now enforcing His victory by collecting the spoils from His victorious war. We are His reward, presented to Him as a gift from the Father.

## The Heavenly Hymns to the Lamb

When the elders and the four creatures fell down before Jesus in John's vision, they started to sing a song of worship to the Lamb of God. This song explains why Jesus is worthy to open the scroll and reveal the secret of the gospel to us:

*And they sang a new song, saying: "You are worthy to take the scroll and to open its seals, because you were slain, and with your blood you purchased for God persons from every tribe and language and people and nation. You have made them to be a kingdom and priests to serve our God, and they will reign on the earth" (Rev. 5:9-10 NIV).*

Jesus is worthy because of his redemptive work on the cross. He purchased us with His blood and made us into a Kingdom of priests. We have now received delegated authority from heaven to reign with Jesus on earth (Luke 10:17-20). This revelation is so glorious that the angel armies join in the worship of the Lamb. They praise Jesus with this powerful hymn: *"Worthy is the Lamb, who was slain, to receive power and wealth and wisdom and strength and honor and glory and praise" (Rev. 5:12 NIV).*

Finally, all of creation will burst forth in worship to the Father and to Jesus Christ, the Lamb of God. *"Then I heard every creature in heaven and on earth and under the earth and on the sea, and all that is in them, saying: "To him who sits on the throne and to the Lamb be praise and honor and glory and power, for ever and ever" (Rev. 5:13 NIV).* All creation will worship the Lamb because He was willing to lay down His life for our sake. Jesus won an eternal victory on the cross, and this made Him worthy to open the scroll and break the seven seals. This causes the people of God from every nation, tribe, and language, throughout all times and ages to proclaim: *"Salvation belongs to our God, who sits on the throne, and to the Lamb" (Rev. 7:9-10 NIV).*

## Behold the Lamb of God!

*"Behold! The Lamb of God who takes away the sin of the world! This is He of whom I said, 'After me comes a Man who is preferred before me, for He was before me.' I did not know Him; but that He should be revealed to Israel, therefore I came baptizing with water" (John 1:29-31 NKJV).* God had given John the Baptist the assignment to prepare the way for Jesus, who came to take away the sins of the world. Jesus became the sacrificial Lamb of heaven who bought us with His blood. In this world, greatness and influence is achieved by overcoming and conquering other people. But in the Kingdom of God, this is always achieved by laying down one's life to serve. Jesus illustrated this in a complete way. His leadership style did not change after His resurrection. Jesus is still the Lamb of God and He still washes our feet and lays down His life for us.

## Washed by the Blood of the Lamb

The blood of the Lamb washes us totally clean from all sins and impurities. It has provided full forgiveness and redemption for us (Eph. 1:7). This means that our innocence has been restored through the finished work of Jesus Christ. In his vision, John sees the spiritual reality of the believers who have been cleansed by the blood of Jesus. This is how we look in the spirit:

*Then one of the elders responded, saying to me, "These who are clothed in the white robes, who are they, and where have they come from?" I said to him, "My lord, you know." And he said to me, "These are the ones who come out of the great tribulation, and they have washed their robes and made them white in the blood of the Lamb" (Rev. 7:13-14 NASB).*

Jesus is our Passover Lamb who delivered us from death (1 Cor. 5:7). In the same way that the people of Israel were saved from destruction and delivered from slavery because of the blood on their door post, so we are saved, healed, and delivered through the blood of Jesus. The Word of God shows us that we have not been purchased with corruptible things like gold or silver "... *but with the precious blood of Christ, a lamb without blemish or defect. He was chosen before the creation of the world, but was revealed in these last times for your sake" (1 Pet. 1:19-20 NIV).*

## The Lamb Who Was Slain Before the Foundation of the World

Jesus was not God's alternate plan because of the fall. The cross of Christ had been the Father's plan all along. He knew from the beginning that we would fall into sin, but He still chose us as His children (Eph. 1:4). Our failures never come as a surprise to God. Jesus became God's solution even before our had sin become the problem. *"And all the people who belong to this world worshiped the beast. They are the ones whose names were not written in the Book of Life that belongs to the Lamb who was slaughtered before the world was made" (Rev. 13:8 NLT).* Jesus came into this world at a certain point in time, but God had decided that this would take place even before He created the world.

We don't have to fear our future failures and sins. The Father has already planned how to make all things work for our good (Rom. 8:28). Jesus will never be ashamed or afraid of our failures, and neither is He threatened or nervous because of our sins. Sin has no power over Him. It is a defeated enemy, and we have been delivered from its power through Jesus Christ. Therefore, we are now fully forgiven and totally set free from all condemnation. *"In whom we have redemption through his blood, the forgiveness of sins, according to the riches of his grace; wherein he hath abounded toward us in all wisdom and prudence" (Eph. 1:7-8).* All our sins have been nailed to the cross and our guilt has been removed (Col. 2:13-15).

The best way I know to express this reality is that the Father took our stupidity factor into the equation when He saved us. Jesus has set us free from sin, once and for all. It is through a revelation and proclamation of the blood of the Lamb that we overcome the realm of darkness. *"For the accuser of our brothers and sisters has been thrown down to earth— the one who accuses them before our God day and night. And they have defeated him by the blood of the Lamb and by their testimony. And they did not love their lives so much that they were afraid to die" (Rev. 12:10-11 NLT).*

### The Lamb is Our Shepherd

Later we will look a little deeper into Jesus' ministry as our good Shepherd, but here we can see that His ministry as our Shepherd is connected to Him being the Lamb of God. Few people have ever heard of a Lamb who shepherds people, but that is exactly what Jesus does. *"They will no longer hunger nor thirst, nor will the sun beat down on them, nor any scorching heat; for the Lamb in the center of the throne will be their shepherd, and will guide them to springs of the water of life; and God will wipe every tear from their eyes"* (Rev. 7:16-17 NASB). He will guide us to the springs of life-giving water where we can drink from the presence of the Holy Spirit. It is important that we eat the rich dishes from the Word of God, but we need to drink the living water of the Holy Spirit as well. Otherwise, our spiritual life will become dry. The water of life makes our hearts soft. Jesus Himself will wipe away our tears and comfort us when we are going through seasons of pain.

An important part of the ministry of Jesus is to bring comfort and healing to His bride. He is the safest person in the universe for us to go to with our pain and brokenness. He heals and restores completely!

**Activations**

- Set apart 20-30 minutes for prayer. Ask the Holy Spirit to reveal the meekness and loving kindness of the Lamb of God to you. Ask Him to reveal the self-giving love of Jesus in a deeper way. Write down what He reveals to you.

- Pray and meditate over the fact that Jesus indwells you. How does it change your life with God to know Christ in you? Ask Jesus to remove anything in your life that hinders His life from flowing through you. Jesus wants to shine forth through every area of your life.

- In this chapter I wrote that the Father took your stupidity factor into the equation when He saved you. Your sins have already been washed away by the blood of Jesus. Ask the Holy Spirit for deeper revelation on this reality. Write down the insights and revelation that you receive.

- Invite Jesus to deliver you from condemnation and sin-consciousness, so that you can live a life of freedom and boldness. Spend time with Jesus in prayer and ask Him to reveal areas in your life where you might still be living under guilt and condemnation. Invite Jesus to minister to these areas so that you can step into more freedom.

# CHAPTER 3: THE MEEKNESS OF THE LAMB

There is something important to be said about the humility and lovingkindness of Jesus. As I mentioned earlier, knowing Jesus as the Lamb of God has brought a lot of healing to my heart and filled my soul with peace. Many of the leadership models of this world promote the self-assured and strong leader, who gains a following by self-promotion and charisma. In the political world, it has become more important to be charismatic and well-spoken than to have real substance and character. Religion operates in a similar fashion, creating harsh and arrogant leaders, who are full of false humility. Jesus turns these corrupt models of leadership on its head. He leads in kindness and humility. This has been an important revelation for me. When I came to Christ I was broken and full of fear but my heart was healed when I encountered the gentleness of Jesus. The following passage of scripture shows us the spirit in which the Lamb of God leads.

*Take a careful look at my servant, my chosen one. I love him dearly and I find all my delight in him. I will breathe my Spirit upon him and he will decree justice to the nations. He will not quarrel or raise his voice in public. He won't brush aside the bruised and broken. He will be gentle with the weak and feeble, until his victory releases justice. And the fame of his name will birth hope among the people (Matt. 12:18-21 TPT).*

## The Beast and the Power of Satan

Jesus always leads His people in gentleness and humility, which is one of the reasons why He is described as the Lamb of God. In the book of Revelation, the evil leadership that receives authority from Satan is described as the beast. *"And the whole earth was amazed and followed after the beast; they worshiped the dragon because*

*he gave his authority to the beast; and they worshiped the beast, saying, 'Who is like the beast, and who is able to wage war with him'" (Rev. 13:3-4 NASB)?* In the book of Revelation, the beast serves as a contrast to the Lamb, and all throughout the Bible, evil powers as well as authoritarian leadership are commonly referred to as beasts (Dan. 4:2-8). These demonic powers conquer through fear and control, forcing people into obedience. This is the nature of the devil. He cannot understand the way of the Lamb, which was the reason that he couldn't foresee God's plan with the cross.
He has no concept of sacrificial love, so he couldn't understand how Jesus could win by laying down His life in humility (1 Cor. 2:6-8). The devil participated in his own defeat when he caused the religious leaders in Israel to persecute and kill Jesus. Satan thought that he could overcome Jesus through fear and control, but divine love always casts out fear. The self-giving love of Jesus overcame the power of the devil on the cross, which reveals that the gentleness and kindness of the Lamb is stronger than the power of the beast.

### The Lamb is Gentle and Humble in Heart

The Lamb of God was slain to deliver us through His blood. Jesus came as a servant, who laid down His life to redeem us. The more we encounter the heart of the Lamb, the more we will realize that He is the kindest and gentlest person in the whole universe. *"Take my yoke upon you, and learn of me; for I am meek and lowly in heart: and ye shall find rest unto your souls. For my yoke is easy, and my burden is light" (Matt. 11:29-30).* We live in a world in which we have been taught to win by being competitive and by making sure we get ahead in life. But that is not the way of the Lamb. In the Word of God, the lamb is a picture of innocence and purity (Luke 10:3). This is the opposite of being ruthless or competitive. In the Kingdom of God, the strength and wisdom of this world is foolishness and weakness. *"For the "foolish" things of God have proven to be wiser than human wisdom. And the "feeble" things of God have proven to be far more powerful than any human ability"* (1 Cor. 1:25 TPT). As we continue to grow into the image of Christ, we will learn to walk in the humility and gentleness of the Lamb, who expresses Himself in a lifestyle of sacrificial love.

## Jesus Humbled Himself for Our Sake

Jesus demonstrated what divine love looks like. It is a self-giving love that always humbles itself to lift other people. Divine love always lays down its own rights to serve its neighbor.

*In your relationships with one another, have the same mindset as Christ Jesus: Who, being in very nature God, did not consider equality with God something to be used to his own advantage; rather, he made himself nothing by taking the very nature of a servant, being made in human likeness (Phil. 2:5-7 NIV).*

We are called to have the same mindset as Jesus did, but we can't achieve that by spiritual disciplines or through will power. It can only be accomplished by a transforming work of grace through the power of the Holy Spirit. As we abide in Christ, our lives will be shaped by His, so that people can see Jesus through us. It is by growing in revelation of His love, that we will learn to love as He loves. Jesus shows us with His own life what divine love looks like. His sacrifice on the cross proves how deeply He was willing humble Himself to save us. *"And being found in appearance as a man, he humbled himself by becoming obedient to death— even death on a cross" (Phil. 2:8 NIV)!* This is still true today. The Son of man did not come for us to serve Him, but He came to serve us (Matt. 20:28). Jesus does not need us, but He loves us and wants to live in fellowship with us. Studying the fruit of the Spirit and the Beatitudes show us what the character of the Lamb looks like. These are more than just good character traits. They reveal the nature and mindset of the Lamb, showing us what a beautiful Savior and friend He is.

## The Fruit of the Spirit

The fruit of the Spirit grows in our union with Christ because it is the nature of Jesus.  Since we have become partakers of divine nature, the fruit of the Spirit is our true nature as well (2 Pet. 1:4). Fruit will manifest as we abide in His love. We find these fruits in Paul's letter to the Galatians: *"But the fruit of the Spirit is love, joy, peace, patience, kindness, goodness, faithfulness, gentleness, self-control; against such things there is no law" (Gal. 5:22-24 NASB).*
It is worth noticing that that the fruit of the Spirit is mentioned in singular here. This is because these fruits are all expressions of the love of the Father. When we abide in His love, our character will be conformed into that of Jesus. We cannot produce the fruit of the Spirit by ourselves, but it will grow in our fellowship with Jesus. As we abide in Him, He will conform us into His image.

## The Fruit of the Spirit Reveal the Nature of the Lamb

I have always been very fascinated by the fruit of the Spirit. It shows us who God is. To know that He is kind and patient makes it easier to trust Him and His plan for my life. Probably one of the best and simplest description of this fruit that I have seen, is found in the Passion Translation.

*"But the fruit produced by the Holy Spirit within you is divine love in all its varied expressions: joy that overflows, peace that subdues, patience that endures, kindness in action, a life full of virtue, faith that prevails, gentleness of heart, and strength of spirit. Never set the law above these qualities, for they are meant to be limitless" (Gal. 5:22-23 TPT).*

We will now take a brief look at each one of these fruits to study how they reveal the mindset and nature of Jesus in a clear and simple way:

- *Divine love in all its varied expressions.* God is love and everything He is and does, will always be an expression of divine love. Christlike character is always a fruit of the love of God transforming our heart. All transformation and discipleship must be rooted in knowing that we love Him because He first loved us (1 John 4:19).

- *Joy that overflows.* Jesus was anointed with the oil of joy more than all of us (Hebr. 1:9). Jesus shows us that a lifestyle of sanctification is a joyful lifestyle. As we abide in Christ, the joy of God will overflow until it breaks the yoke of heaviness and heals our wounded soul. The fruit of joy reveals God's perspective and establishes us in His victory. We can handle anything we face in life when we have the fruit of joy.

- *Peace that subdues.* Jesus is the Prince of Peace. Peace means harmony and wholeness. Jesus gave His own peace to us, which means that we can freely partake of the harmony and wholeness of heaven (John 14:27). The peace of heaven subdues all stress and delivers us from the need of being in control. It overcomes every spiritual attack and breaks the power of the devil. Jesus has done everything for us so that we can walk in harmony and joy in all of life's circumstances. Living in the peace of God means that we walk in wholeness and completeness in every area of our lives.

- *Patience that endures.* Jesus will never change and His character is constantly the same. Jesus is unchangeable and He is not influenced by surrounding circumstances. That is patience in action. Most of us have had lots of opportunities to experience this personally. Jesus is very patient with us. He has been waiting for at least two thousand years for His bride to mature, and He will keep on waiting patiently until we are where He wants us to be. As we grow in the fruit of patience, we will learn to endure, knowing that God's will is coming to pass.

While we are still waiting for that to happen, we can remain in character, being unfazed by what's going on around us. That is the fruit of patience in action!

- *Kindness in action.* Jesus is the kindest person in the universe. Being kind means being flexible and easy to get along with. The love of the Father is always kind.
  The more we grow in Christlikeness, the kinder we will be with people, especially with the ones with whom we disagree and who challenge us the most. Encountering the kindness of Jesus is a very healing experience, and as we grow in the kindness of God, people will find us easy to get along with.

- *A life full of virtue.* Jesus is full of virtue, always serving people without selfish motives and hidden agendas.
  He always has the best interest of others on His heart and His motives are always pure. That is the definition of goodness. God is always good and we grow in goodness and purity of heart by getting to know and experience His goodness. As we are doing that, we will live out that goodness toward other people as well, serving them by having their best interest in our heart.

- *Faith that prevails.* Jesus demonstrates prevailing faith in all His dealings with us because we are saved by His faithfulness. He will never change and He will always be true to His promises. This will also become our character the more we are conformed into His likeness.

- *Gentleness of heart.* Jesus is a gentleman, who treat both His bride and His enemies, with patience and kindness. Jesus is full of humility. As we are being conformed into His image and get a deeper revelation of His heart, we will also be growing in humility and gentleness toward people.

- *Strength of spirit.* Jesus never controls people, but He is always walking in self-control. This is the reason that He never reacts to the actions of other people, but always acts according to the Father's plan (John 5:19). Walking in self-control means that we are only doing what we see Him doing. That is to be strong in Spirit.

These expressions of divine love describe the character of Jesus and since we are partakers of His nature, they describe who we really are as well. They describe what the New Creation lifestyle looks like. When we spend time with Jesus, the fruit of the Spirit will grow in our lives.

## The Beatitudes

Another important teaching in the Bible that reveal the way of the Lamb is the sermon on the mount, particularly the opening statements of this teaching, the Beatitudes. Jesus declares that the one who possesses the character traits mentioned within them are blessed. This means that such people are happy and blissful. When teaching these Beatitudes, Jesus is showing us who He is and how He relates to His Father. Since they describe the nature of Jesus, they reveal our true nature as well. The transforming work of grace in our lives, breaks the old fleshly patterns so that we can walk according to who we are, which is reflected in these Beatitudes.

### *Blessed are the poor in spirit: for theirs is the kingdom of heaven (Matt. 5:3)*

Jesus is the Son of God, and yet, while He walked on this earth, He lived in utter dependence upon His Father (John 5:19). This is the essence of being poor in spirit. We are poor in spirit when we realize how much we need to depend on God. We need His love and mercy everyday of our lives. Spiritual poverty means to long for more revelation and encounters with the Father. There is always much more for us to experience when it comes to our inheritance in Christ. There are no professionals in the Kingdom of God. We will always have more to learn together with Jesus.

### *Blessed are they that mourn: for they shall be comforted (Matt. 5:4)*

Jesus mourned and wept over Jerusalem. He mourned the state of humanity because of the fall to the point that He became a man of sorrows to bring redemption and healing for the wound of sin (Isa. 53:1-5). Since it requires a soft heart, being able to mourn is a great blessing. A lot of people have hardened their heart as a way of surviving the pain of life. Consequently, they have now become numb and lost connection with their brokenness. God is the God of all comfort and Jesus constantly showers us with His comforting love, wiping every tear from our eyes. He longs to heal our broken heart (2 Cor. 1:3-6, Phil. 2:1).

*Blessed are the meek: for they shall inherit the earth
(Matt. 5:5)*

Meekness and gentleness are the disposition of Jesus' own heart
(Matt. 11:29). Being meek means being gentle and flexible toward
both God and man. When we give up our rights, realizing that
all that we have belongs to God, we can live in a gentle and mild
manner. The one who does not claim anything as his own, will
receive everything from the Father. This is a good description of
living in meekness and humility. Biblical meekness looks like
Jesus giving up His life and dying on the cross to redeem us from
our sins.

*Blessed are they which do hunger and thirst after righteousness:
for they shall be filled (Matt. 5:6)*

Jesus is the King of righteousness and when the Kingdom comes
it means that the reign of God and the righteousness of Christ is
being established. For us to hunger and thirst after righteousness
means to long for Christlikeness, so that we can see more of the
Kingdom of God manifest through us. His power will manifest
in this world as Jesus is revealed through our lives.

*Blessed are the merciful: for they shall obtain mercy (Matt. 5:7)*

Jesus is a merciful High Priest who showers us with His grace
(Hebr. 2:17). He wants us to love mercy because that is what the
Father does (Micah 6:8). Mercy means that we don't get what we
deserve when we sin, so loving mercy is to have a heart that long
to forgive and restore the one who is guilty. We have all fallen
short and sinned. We rightfully deserved to be punished for our
sins, but Jesus took our punishment so that we could go free. This
is mercy! We need to take every chance we get to pass it on.

***Blessed are the pure in heart: for they shall see God (Matt. 5:8)***

Jesus is pure in heart. Purity of heart is closely associated to being good and it means living without secret agendas and hidden motives before both God and men. We are called to live without falsehood or selfishness by sacrificially loving both God and our neighbor. When our hearts are pure, we will grow into a clear revelation of who the Father is. This is the reason why the Father wants us to become like children. The innocence of the childlike heart sets us free from being motivated by selfish gain and lust for power. This is the foundation for intimacy with Jesus because only the pure in heart can see God as He truly is.

***Blessed are the peacemakers: for they shall be called the children of God (Matt. 5:9)***

Jesus is the Prince of Peace and His Kingdom is built on joy, peace and righteousness in the Holy Spirit (Rom. 14:17). Jesus gave us peace with God by reconciling us to the Father. Jesus is the great peacemaker. Being a peacemaker means being ready to do whatever we can to reconcile relationships and create a life in harmony with our neighbor. To do this, we need to be willing to give up our need to have the last word. We are called to take the first step in settling disagreements and healing relationships.
A peacemaker is ready to turn the other cheek and walk the extra mile for this to happen (Matt. 5:39-42).

***Blessed are they which are persecuted for righteousness' sake: for theirs is the kingdom of heaven (Matt. 5:10)***

Jesus had to endure a lot of persecution throughout His ministry (John 15:18-22). The revelation of the heart of the Father and the grace of God that flowed through His life was too much for the religious leaders to handle. We are living in a fallen world and we will be persecuted for righteousness' sake at times. Anyone who lives in an intimate relationship with Jesus becomes a threat to the devil, and he will instigate persecution toward that person. Being persecuted for a bad character or bad attitudes brings no reward at all, but being persecuted for Jesus' sake will make us inherit the Kingdom of heaven (1 Pet. 2:19-20).

## Beholding Jesus in the Scriptures

As we are studying the Beatitudes and the fruit of the Spirit, we can see how they reveal the heart of the Lamb. We have received a promise that real and lasting transformation will happen as we behold Jesus Christ. Seeing Him in the Scriptures is one of the ways in which we do that:

*We can all draw close to him with the veil removed from our faces. And with no veil we all become like mirrors who brightly reflect the glory of the Lord Jesus. We are being transfigured into his very image as we move from one brighter level of glory to another. And this glorious transfiguration comes from the Lord, who is the Spirit (2 Cor. 3:18 TPT).*

We have looked at the nature of the Lamb by studying the fruit of the Spirit and the Beatitudes. Since we have been made a New Creation and are partakers of divine nature, both the Beatitudes and the fruit of the Spirit reveal who we really are. It is a healing experience to encounter the meek and gentle Lamb of God. He is the kindest and most loving person in the universe, and we have been given the awesome privilege to call Him our Savior and Friend.

# Activations

- Set aside 20-30 minutes for prayer. Ask the Holy Spirit to reveal more about how Jesus leads us in meekness and gentleness. Read Matt. 12:18-21 together with the Holy Spirit to gain more insight into this topic. How will this affect how you live and minister to people? Write down what the Holy Spirit reveals to you.

- In this chapter, we saw that the beast stands in contrast to the Lamb. Read the passages in the book of Revelation that describe the Lamb and the beast (Rev. 5:1-14, 7:13-17, 13:1-18, 14:1-5). Read them prayerfully together with the Holy Spirit and invite Him to give deeper insight on the nature and leadership of the Lamb and the beast. How are they different?

- Read the passages from the Bible about the fruit of the Spirit and the beatitudes again (Gal. 5:22-23, Matt. 5:1-10). Read them slowly and prayerfully several times and ask the Holy Spirit to reveal the character of the Lamb in these texts. To encounter Jesus in this way brings healing to our heart.

- Take some time to pray and reflect on how you can live and minister to people in a way that is according to the heart of the Lamb. Ask Jesus to reveal His heart through your life every day.

# CHAPTER 4: THE BRIDE OF THE LAMB

In an earlier chapter we saw how the eyes of Jesus Christ burns with flames of life-giving fire while He is looking at His bride. They burn with His holy love and passion for us. This should not come as a surprise since we are His bride. *"And I John saw the holy city, new Jerusalem, coming down from God out of heaven, prepared as a bride adorned for her husband"* (Rev. 21:2). Oftentimes, we refer to the church as the bride of Christ, which is an accurate statement because we are. But we are never called that in the Bible. Instead, we are called the bride, and the wife of the Lamb (Rev. 21:9). It is powerful to know that the Lamb of God is our Bridegroom and that we are living in a union of love with Him forever!

**The Wedding Feast of the Lamb**

The book of Revelation speaks about the marriage of the Lamb and the wedding feast taking place in celebration of the union between Jesus and His bride.

*"Let's rejoice and be glad and give the glory to Him, because the marriage of the Lamb has come, and His bride has prepared herself." It was given to her to clothe herself in fine linen, bright and clean; for the fine linen is the righteous acts of the saints. Then he said to me, "Write: 'Blessed are those who are invited to the wedding feast of the Lamb"* (Rev. 19:8-9 NASB).

This marriage might be a future event, but on a deeper level it is describing the reality of us being united with Jesus Christ right now (Rom. 6:1-11). In that sense, we are presently living in the wedding feast of the Lamb, where we can enjoy all the fullness of God in Christ. There are unsearchable riches in Christ, and they are all available for us to explore right now. The treasure that we have received in Christ is so vast that we will explore it for all eternity. Right now, the bride of Jesus is maturing and growing into the full manifestation of her bridal identity. But we are still the bride right now.

## We are the New Jerusalem

The observant reader noticed how the New Jerusalem that came down from heaven was prepared as a bride for her husband. We are not only called the bride of the Lamb, but we are called the New Jerusalem as well. Here is another passage, describing the same reality:

*"Come here, I will show you the bride, the wife of the Lamb." And he carried me away in the Spirit to a great and high mountain, and showed me the holy city, Jerusalem, coming down out of heaven from God, having the glory of God. Her brilliance was like a very valuable stone, like a stone of crystal-clear jasper" (Rev. 21:9-11 NASB).*

The angel carried John to a high mountain to show him the wife of the Lamb. As the angel pointed to the bride, John saw the New Jerusalem descending from heaven. The bride and the city of God are one and the same. The church is the New Jerusalem, but we are the wife of the Lamb as well. This is not speaking of future events but point to who we are in Christ. We are now the wife of the Lamb and the New Jerusalem. In a later chapter we will study this revelation in greater depths, but the important thing for us to understand right now is that Jesus has already been united with His beloved bride, which is us!

**Experiential Union**

Jesus is deeply in love with His people and He will do whatever it takes to win our hearts. Jesus' deepest longing is for His bride to be fully His. We are already united to Jesus by faith, but He wants us to live in an experiential union of love with Him as well. Jesus wants to have all of us, and He longs for our affection and adoration. It has been the Father's plan from the beginning to present a mature, holy and spotless bride to Jesus as a gift.

This is the reason that the Holy Spirit is doing a transforming work within us (Rom. 8:29). The ministry of the Holy Spirit is all about maturing the bride of Christ by revealing the beauty of our Bridegroom. The more we see who Jesus is, the more we will fall in love with Him. Because Jesus is so passionate about His bride, there are many types and shadows revealing the love of Christ for His bride throughout the Scriptures, and we will find the first one right at the beginning.

**Jesus is the Second Adam**

*"So also it is written: "The first man, Adam, became a living person." The last Adam was a life-giving spirit" (1 Cor. 15:45).* Jesus is called the second Adam because He redeemed the failures of the first Adam. Jesus Christ healed and restored everything that had been damaged and lost through the fall. At the same time, Adam is also a type of Christ. Adam was brought to life within the garden of Eden, where he fellowshipped with God every day. He knew nothing about sin, death or evil. Even in this state of bliss and perfection, Adam was alone: *"The Lord God said, "It is not good for the man to be alone. I will make a helper suitable for him" (Gen. 2:18 NIV).*

Even though God had created all kinds of living creatures, Adam was still lonely, because there was no other human being that was like him among them. It was then that God decided to create His most beautiful creation - the woman. *"So the Lord God caused a deep sleep to fall upon the man, and he slept; then He took one of his ribs and closed up the flesh at that place. And the Lord God fashioned into a woman the rib which He had taken from the man, and brought her to the man"* (Gen. 2:21-22 NASB). When Adam woke from his sleep, he was introduced to Eve. She could balance him and be his counterpart in all things. *"Then the man said, "At last this is bone of my bones, And flesh of my flesh; She shall be called 'woman,' Because she was taken out of man." For this reason, a man shall leave his father and his mother, and be joined to his wife; and they shall become one flesh* (Gen. 2:23-24 NASB). Eve had been taken out of Adam's side and she became his beloved wife and equal. Adam was no longer alone.

Adam and Eve enjoyed a relationship of complete harmony and love. They were naked and unashamed before one another. They did not yet have a concept of shame or rejection. *"And the man and his wife were both naked, but they were not ashamed"* (Gen. 2:25 *NASB)*. This changed after the fall, but their relationship prior to this, revealed the Father's original plan for man and woman.

The relationship between Adam and Eve is a powerful picture of Jesus and His bride. Jesus wanted a counterpart, someone who could complete Him. Through His redemptive work on the cross Jesus won us as His bride. Just like Eve was taken out of the side of man, so the bride of Christ was brought forth from His side, which was pierced by the soldier's spear. *"Yet one of the soldiers pierced His side with a spear, and immediately blood and water came out"* (John 19:34 NASB). When Jesus was pierced and blood and water flowed out of His side, the bride of Christ was brought forth. We are now flesh of His flesh, and bone of His bone, united with Him in a union of love for all eternity.

## Marriage Is a Picture of Christ and His Church

This is the reason that the marriage between husband and wife is a picture of Christ and His church. *"For this reason a man shall leave his father and his mother and be joined to his wife, and the two shall become one flesh. This mystery is great; but I am speaking with reference to Christ and the church" (Eph. 5:31-32 NASB).* Marriage is such a big deal to God because it speaks of Jesus and His bride. The union between a husband and a wife point to our union with Jesus Christ. When God declares that He hates divorce, it is not to condemn the person who has lost his or her marriage (Mal. 2:16). He wants to reassure us that divorce and separation is not part of His nature. Jesus will never leave us, no matter how badly we mess up. He does not have abandonment within His nature and nothing can separate us from His love. *"For I am convinced that neither death, nor life, nor angels, nor principalities, nor things present, nor things to come, nor powers, nor height, nor depth, nor any other created thing will be able to separate us from the love of God that is in Christ Jesus our Lord" (Rom 8:38-39 NASB).*

## We Are United with Christ

When a man and a woman marry and consummate the marriage by being intimate together, they become one flesh. In the same way, we have now become one body with Jesus Christ (Rom. 6:1-8, 1 Cor. 12:27, Col. 3:15). In fact, our union with Jesus goes much deeper than even the best earthly marriage because we are now one spirit with Him. *"Do you not know that your bodies are parts of Christ…But the one who joins himself to the Lord is one spirit with Him" (1 Cor. 6:15, 17 NASB).* We are the bride and Jesus is our Bridegroom. We are now united with Him forever through the cross. The New Covenant has been sealed by His own blood, and it will never change or be dissolved! *"Wherefore, my brethren, ye also are become dead to the law by the body of Christ; that ye should be married to another, even to him who is raised from the dead, that we should bring forth fruit unto God" (Rom. 7:4).*

## The Friend of the Bridegroom

John the Baptist was called the friend of the Bridegroom. When John was sent ahead of Jesus to proclaim that the long-awaited Messiah finally was about to arrive, he was sent to prepare the way for Jesus to win a bride for Himself. John has this to say about his relationship to Jesus. *"The bride belongs to the bridegroom. The friend who attends the bridegroom waits and listens for him, and Is full of joy when he hears the bridegroom's voice. That joy is mine, and it is now complete. He must become greater; I must become less" (John 3:29-30 NIV).* When the Bridegroom arrived, John knew that his job was done, and that made his joy full. As Jesus started His ministry, Jesus had to increase, while John was decreasing.

## The Love Story Is Foreshadowed

The story of Jesus and His bride is foreshadowed by prophetic types all throughout the Old Testament. We have already seen how Adam and Eve is a type of Christ and the church, but there are many other prophetic types to be found in the Old Testament as well. Throughout this book, we are going to look at several of these pictures. In ending this chapter, we will look briefly at two couples that are both obvious and wonderful examples of Jesus and His bride.

## Isaac and Rebekah

The story of Isaac and Rebekah is one of the clearest pictures of Jesus and His bride in the Scriptures (Gen. 24:1-66). In this story, Isaac is a type of Jesus. Isaac is the seed of Abraham, the son of promise. In His letter to the Galatians, Paul shows how Jesus is the true seed of Abraham: *"Now to Abraham and his seed were the promises made. He saith not, and to seeds, as of many; but as of one, And to thy seed, which is Christ"* (Gal. 3:16). Abraham is a type of the Father, since He desires for His son to have a bride and sends a servant to find her in a foreign country. That servant is a type of the Holy Spirit who is sent by the Father to find and prepare a bride for the Son. Rebekah is a picture of the bride of Jesus Christ. The union between Isaac and Rebekah becomes fruitful and their offspring brings salvation into this world through the birth of Christ. Our union with Jesus becomes fruitful as well. Through our relationship with Jesus, salvation will go forth everywhere.

## Joseph Takes a Gentile Bride

In a similar way, Joseph the grandson of Isaac, is a picture of Christ. Just like Jesus, He was his father's favorite son (Matt. 3:16-17). Joseph was betrayed and sold by his brothers, but their betrayal enabled him to save them from death. Joseph was raised into a place of authority and he forgave His brothers, not holding their transgressions against them. When the brothers met Joseph in Egypt, they did not recognize him at first, just like the Jewish people does not recognize Jesus as their Messiah (2 Cor. 3:12-18). After Joseph ascended into a position of authority to rule, he was presented with a gentile bride as a gift. *"Then Pharaoh named Joseph Zaphenath-paneah; and he gave him Asenath, the daughter of Potiphera priest of On, to be his wife. And Joseph went out over the land of Egypt"* (Gen. 41:45 NASB). This is a prophetic picture of Jesus being presented with a gentile bride as a gift from His Heavenly Father (John 17:6). When we grow in our revelation of Jesus as our Bridegroom, our hearts will be filled with devotion and adoration of the Lamb. He longs for intimate union with his people (1 Cor. 1:9).

## The Romance of the Ages

The story of Jesus and His bride is the romance of the ages. Every love story that we find in the Bible is written as a type of this ultimate romance between Jesus and His beloved bride. The love of Jesus has transformed my life just as much as the love of the Father has done. His love is the passionate fire that we call the first love and that is expressed as the fires of revival. Just like the love of the Father provides sonship and identity, the bridal love of Jesus Christ provides romance, passion and it adds a radical wildness to our life with God. We need to be baptized in the love of Jesus Christ again and again if we want to be the radical lovers that we are called to be.

# Activations

- Set aside 20-30 minutes in prayer. Read the Scriptures in this chapter from the book of Revelation that is speaking of us as His beloved bride (Rev. 19:8-9, 21:2, 9-11). Ask the Holy Spirit to reveal your bridal identity in a deeper way. Write down what He reveals to you.

- We are now one body and one spirit with Jesus Himself. This means that you are fully united with Him, and that you are so close to Him that you cannot be separated. Spend some time with Jesus and invite Him to show you how this union changes your relationship with Him.

- Ask Jesus to immerse you in His love for you. The bridal love of Jesus Christ is full of passion and fire. Ask Him to fill your heart with that love, so that you can walk in your bridal identity.

- We have looked briefly at three couples from the Old Testament who are prophetic pictures of Jesus and His bride. Find three more pictures of Jesus and His bride in the Bible. Ask the Holy Spirit to give revelation of your bridal identity through these prophetic pictures.

# CHAPTER 5: THE BRIDE IS THE NEW JERUSALEM

Throughout this book we are looking into the eternal love story of Jesus and His bride. We have seen that we are the bride of the Lamb. This means that we have now been united with Jesus, so that we can live in the fullness of our inheritance today. Jesus speaks of the bride as the New Jerusalem. Since we are the bride, we are also portrayed as the city of God in the book of Revelation. *"Come here, I will show you the bride, the wife of the Lamb." And he carried me away in the Spirit to a great and high mountain, and showed me the holy city, Jerusalem, coming down out of heaven from God, having the glory of God (Rev. 21:9-11 NASB).* When we realize that the New Jerusalem is the bride of Christ, the book of Revelation and other parts of the Scriptures opens in a new way. We have been born from above and we are anointed with the Holy Spirit. We are the City of God, who came down from heaven to steward the glory of God on the earth (Rev. 21:1-3).

### The New Jerusalem & Our Bridal Identity

We are now going to study the New Jerusalem to learn about our identity as the bride of Christ. There are many glorious realities of the New Creation revealed in the description of this Holy City. Much have been written about the symbols and numbers of this city, but here we are going to focus on what the New Jerusalem reveals about our union with Jesus.

- ***The twelve gates and the name of the twelve tribes represent the whole body of Christ.*** *"It had a massive, high wall with twelve gates, and each gate had an angel. Each gate had written upon it a name of one of the twelve tribes of Israel—three gates on the east, three gates on the north, three gates on the south, and three gates on the west" (Rev. 21:12-*

*13 NASB).* Since Israel was divided into twelve tribes, the gates with the names of the twelve tribes are a picture of the New Jerusalem being made up of the whole body of Christ. All the tribes of the church are important because they reveal different parts of Jesus to the world. The gate of each tribe speaks of their ministry to bring people into the Kingdom of God, showing us that every tribe can bring people to Jesus by revealing a unique expression of Christ to the world. We are the new Israel, and the city of God is built of the whole body of Christ (Gal. 6:16).

- ***The City is built upon apostolic foundations.*** *"The city wall had twelve foundations, and on them were the names of the twelve apostles of the Lamb" (Rev. 21:14 NASB).*
The bride of Christ is built upon a solid foundation. This foundation is Jesus Himself, and it is laid by the apostolic ministry. Jesus is the foundation and He will always be the chief corner stone, but apostles and prophets are the ministries equipped to be the foundational ministries in the Kingdom of God (Eph. 2:19-20). Therefore, the names of the apostles were written on the twelve foundations.

- ***The city is shaped as a perfect cube, just like the Holy of Holies in the tabernacle of Moses and the temple.*** *"The city is laid out as a square, and its length is as great as the width; and he measured the city with the rod, twelve thousand stadia; its length, width, and height are equal. And he measured its wall, 144 cubits, by human measurements, which are also angelic measurements"(Rev. 21:16-17 NASB).*
That the city is shaped as a cube is symbolic language, comparing the New Jerusalem to the Holy of Holies in the tabernacle. Just like the presence of God dwelt within the Holy of Holies in the Old Covenant, so the presence

of God dwells within us today. Wherever we go, we are carriers of the presence of God. We are called to live in an experiential union with Jesus all the time, so that we can reveal His presence and power to the world. *"We are like common clay jars that carry this glorious treasure within, so that this immeasurable power will be seen as God's, not ours"* (2 Cor. 5:7 TPT).

- ***The City of God is pure gold, decorated with precious stones, revealing that this city is built upon Christ with incorruptible material. It is indestructible.*** *"The material of the wall was jasper; and the city was pure gold, like clear glass. The foundation stones of the city wall were decorated with every kind of precious stone… And the twelve gates were twelve pearls; each one of the gates was a single pearl. And the street of the city was pure gold, like transparent glass"* (Rev. 21:18-19, 21 NASB). The foundation of New Jerusalem is Jesus Himself, and He has built the city with gold, silver, and precious stones. This is the kind of building material that withstands the day of fire. There will come a day when every man's work is tried by fire and how each one has built will be exposed on that day. Because the Holy City is built with gold, silver, and precious stones, when we are tried by fire, we will certainly come forth as pure gold. We are perfected, blessed, and precious like gold. Because of Jesus, fiery trials will only serve to reveal our identity as His precious bride, while at the same time burning away everything else (1 Cor. 3:11-13).

- ***The Father and Jesus is the temple of the city.*** *"I saw no temple in it, for the Lord God the Almighty and the Lamb are its temple"* (Rev 21:22 NASB). Since Jesus Himself is the object of our worship, there is no need for a temple within the city of God. When Jesus had driven out the moneychangers from the temple, He spoke of His body as the temple that was to be ruined and built up again in three days (John 2:19-22). Jesus doesn't live in temples made with hands. He lives within us! *"For God wanted them to know that the riches and glory of Christ are for you Gentiles, too. And this is the secret: Christ lives in you. This gives you assurance of sharing his glory"* (Col. 1:27 NLT).

- ***The glory of God and the Lamb is the light of the city.*** *"And the city has no need of the sun or of the moon to shine on it, for the glory of God has illuminated it, and its lamp is the Lamb"* (Rev. 21:23 NASB). Jesus is the light of the world, and His presence brings revelation and illumination so that we can have a clear spiritual vision. Jesus Himself illuminates our lives with the glory of God. *"Then Jesus spoke to them again, saying, "I am the light of the world. He who follows Me shall not walk in darkness, but have the light of life"* (John 8:12 NKJV).

- ***The Nations will be enlightened by the city and the kings will bless it with wealth.*** *"The nations will walk by its light, and the kings of the earth will bring their glory into it"* (Rev. 21:24 NASB). Because Jesus, who is the light of the world lives inside of us, we have become the light of the world (Matt. 5:14). As Jesus shines through His bride, the nations will receive light and guidance though us. (Isa. 60:2-3).

- ***The gates of the city are always open, and anyone can enter.*** *"In the daytime (for there will be no night there) its gates will never be closed; and they will bring the glory and the honor of the nations into It"* (Rev. 21:25-26 NASB). The gates will never be shut because God has reconciled the world with Himself through Jesus Christ, and anyone can receive Jesus and enter the city. The person who has been washed by the blood of Jesus is an inhabitant of the New Jerusalem (Rev. 22:14).

- ***Those who do not have Jesus are shut out of the city.***"*…and nothing unclean, and no one who practices abomination and lying, shall ever come into it, but only those whose names are written in the Lamb's book of life"(Rev. 21:27 NASB).* The people who refuse to believe in Jesus are not permitted to enter the holy city. Only people who have received Jesus as Lord and Savior can enter the city. No one who chooses to hold fast to the old life will ever be allowed into the body of Christ (John 3:36).

- ***The water of life flows like a river in the middle of the streets.*** *"And he showed me a river of the water of life, clear as crystal, coming from the throne of God and of the Lamb, in the middle of its street" (Rev. 22:1 NASB).* The water of life is the Holy Spirit, and the presence and anointing of the Holy Spirit flows like a river through the streets of the city. This river flows out from the city of God into this world, turning spiritual wastelands and desolate places within this world into the garden of Eden (Ezek. 47:1-12). The river of God brings life and joy wherever it comes gushing forth. This is the river of the Holy Spirit that flows from our innermost being to bring healing and life everywhere. (John 7:37-39).

- ***The tree of life grows in the city, yielding fruit that brings healing to the nations.*** *"On either side of the river was the tree of life, bearing twelve kinds of fruit, yielding its fruit every month; and the leaves of the tree were for the healing of the nations" (Rev. 22:2 NASB).* Jesus is the Tree of Life, and as the nations are turning to Him, they will be healed and restored. Since Jesus indwells us, we have the tree of life in our hearts, and people can taste its fruits and receive healing from its leaves through us. We have been called to make disciples of all nations. That includes bringing healing to the heart of every nation (Isa. 60:1-7).

- ***There are no curses within the city since Jesus reigns.*** *"There will no longer be any curse; and the throne of God and of the Lamb will be in it" (Rev. 22:3 NASB).* The bride of Christ is a curse free zone. Jesus reigns in the city of God and in Him we have been blessed with all the blessings of heaven (Eph. 1:3). Jesus broke and dissolved all curses through the cross. The curse has no access to the bride of Christ (Gal. 3:13-14). We are blessed!

- ***The inhabitants of the city can see his face and they have been marked with his seal.*** *"…his bond-servants will serve Him; they will see His face, and His name will be on their foreheads" (Rev. 22:3-4 NASB).* We have been sealed and sanctified through the one sacrifice of Jesus Christ (Hebr. 10:10-14). We can behold the face of Jesus and see who He really is by beholding His glory whenever we want. We now have access to the full revelation of Jesus Himself (2 Cor. 3:18).

- ***The city is illuminated by God, who has brought the eternal day of salvation.*** *"And there will no longer be any night; and they will not have need of the light of a lamp nor the light of the sun, because the Lord God will illuminate them; and they will reign forever and ever" (Rev. 22:1 NASB).* There is no darkness or night within the city of God. We live in the favorable time and the day of salvation. In the New Covenant there is no mix of light and darkness, and there is no night because the sun of righteousness always shines upon us. We are now living in the everlasting day of breakthrough and favor from the Lord (2 Cor. 6:2).

All these glorious realities that we have studied above, describe who we are in Christ, and we can walk in them here and now. *"I saw the Holy City, the new Jerusalem, coming down out of heaven from God, prepared as a bride beautifully dressed for her husband. And I heard a loud voice from the throne saying, "Look! God's dwelling place is now among the people, and he will dwell with them. They will be his people, and God himself will be with them and be their God" (Rev. 21:2-3 NIV).* We are the Father's dwelling place and Jesus wants to reveal His presence and glory here in this world through us. The book of Revelation is not the only book that speaks of the New Jerusalem. Other parts of the Bible reveal even more about the Holy City. For example, the book of Hebrews contains some very interesting revelations on this topic.

### Mount Zion & the City of the Living God

The New Jerusalem is our eternal dwelling place. We don't have to wait to go there until we die. Since we are the city of God, we have already arrived there. The heavenly places in which we are seated with Christ is located within this heavenly city. We are the New Jerusalem, but the Holy City is our dwelling place as well.

*But you have come to Mount Zion and to the city of the living God, the heavenly Jerusalem, and to myriads of angels, to the general assembly and church of the firstborn who are enrolled in heaven, and to God, the Judge of all, and to the spirits of the righteous made perfect, and to Jesus, the mediator of a new covenant, and to the sprinkled blood, which speaks better than the blood of Abel (Hebr. 12:22-24 NASB).*

We have already looked at Mount Zion earlier in this book. This mountain is the City of God. The Father lives there, since this city is also the Father's house (John 14:1-7). Jesus Christ is the light of the city and His glory always shines there. The atmosphere of the New Jerusalem is saturated with the blood of Jesus. His blood declares forgiveness, peace, freedom, and it testifies to the love of the Father. The armies of angels are there, together with the righteous and perfected church. It is no wonder that the heroes of faith longed for the city of God. They knew that God had made this city their home. *"But now they desire a better country, that is, an heavenly: wherefore God is not ashamed to be called their God: for he hath prepared for them a city" (Hebr. 11:16).* Together with us, these Old Testament saints now inhabit the New Jerusalem.

## The River & the City of God

The city of God appears in the Psalms as well. There we find how the river of the Holy Spirit releases streams that bring joy and delight to the bride of the Lamb.

*God has a constantly flowing river whose sparkling streams bring joy and delight to his people. His river flows right through the city of God Most High, into his holy dwelling places. God is in the midst of his city, secure and never shaken. At daybreak his help will be seen with the appearing of the dawn (Ps 46:4-5 TPT).*

The bride of the Lamb will rejoice when she receives the different streams of life that are flowing from the river of the Holy Spirit. I have asked God many times to be touched and transformed by as many streams of the Holy Spirit as possible. I don't want to miss anything that Jesus is doing in the body of Christ today! This city is the dwelling place of the Godhead. Our morning has dawned and we are living in the day of salvation, meaning that the Holy Spirit, our helper, provides all the support that we need. This city will never ever be shaken or and its foundation will not be moved. We have a sure foundation in Christ!

## Carrying a Vision of the Heavenly City & Enduring the Reproach of Christ

Everyone who lives out their bridal identity will sooner or later be persecuted. This persecution will mostly come from religion and the religious spirit (Gal 4:28-29). Persecution can at times be very painful, but when we carry a revelation of Jesus' love for us, we will find strength and grace to endure and overcome during persecution.

*So also Jesus suffered and died outside the city gates to make his people holy by means of his own blood. So let us go out to him, outside the camp, and bear the disgrace he bore. For this world is not our permanent home; we are looking forward to a home yet to come (Hebr. 13:12-14 NLT).*

If our value system as believers is based on a religious order of church life, the price of suffering the reproach of Christ will be too high. That usually leads the believer to compromise in the name "balance". Religion values political correctness because its adherents want to be accepted. It is important to the legalistic mind to appear respectable. But the one who has been captivated by the love of Jesus Christ knows that our lives are lived in the audience of One. It is a huge honor to share in the reproach of Christ because we're inhabiting the New Jerusalem and releasing heaven on earth.

### Babylon the Great Harlot

When we are speaking of the reproach of Christ, we need to look at the demonic source of this persecution. That source is the religious spirit. In the book of Revelation, the religious spirit is portrayed as a woman, who is also a city. *"And the woman whom you saw is that great city which reigns over the kings of the earth" (Rev.*

*17:18 NKJV)*. In the same way that the beast appears as an evil counterfeit of Jesus Christ, this woman, who is the great city of Babylon, is Satan's perverted version of the bride of the Lamb and the New Jerusalem. This woman whose name is Babylon, the great harlot, is the religious spirit. Her demonic activity focuses on persecuting and ruining the bride of Christ. This is how the book of Revelation describes her war on the saints:

*And on her forehead a name was written: MYSTERY, BABYLON THE GREAT, THE MOTHER OF HARLOTS AND OF THE ABOMINATIONS OF THE EARTH. I saw the woman, drunk with the blood of the saints and with the blood of the martyrs of Jesus (Rev. 17:4-6 NKJV).*

Most believers who were once in love with Jesus, but who have now grown cold, have fallen victim to this spirit. Babylon means *confusion* or *mixture*. We can't mix legalism with the pure grace of Jesus Christ. That is spiritual adultery, which is the reason that the religious spirit is called a harlot. As the bride of Christ, we need to listen to this heavenly exhortation and warning: *"And I heard another voice from heaven saying, "Come out of her, my people, lest you share in her sins, and lest you receive of her plagues" (Rev. 18:5 NKJV).* We have died with Christ to the religious order and we have no part in the religious spirit. Therefore, Jesus calls us to leave the city of confusion and mixture, to make mount Zion our dwelling place instead. Living there means that we are firmly planted in the love of the Father and the finished work of Jesus.

### The End of the Religious Spirit

We know that every enemy is now being placed under the feet of Jesus Christ, and that includes the religious spirit. This spirit is a defeated enemy and even though we have not yet seen the full manifestation of this reality, religion has no power over us.

The religious spirit will soon be destroyed, and all its legalistic teachings and doctrines will perish with it.

*"Hallelujah! Salvation, glory, and power belong to our God, because His judgments are true and righteous; for He has judged the great prostitute who was corrupting the earth with her sexual immorality, and He has avenged the blood of His bond-servants on her." And a second time they said, "Hallelujah! Her smoke rises forever and ever"* (Rev. 19:1-3 NIV).

Jesus Christ has overcome all His enemies, and that includes the religious spirit. The gospel of Jesus Christ will triumph over the religious order and Jesus will become all in all (1 Cor. 15:28). Let's take the journey out of the city of mixture and confusion into the New Jerusalem. The city of God is our home and inheritance!

## The Journey of Abraham

The life of Abraham is an example of how a fresh vision of the New Jerusalem is the beginning of a journey with Jesus, from the familiar into unknown territory. This is a journey that brings us out of religion, and into the promised land. *"By faith Abraham, when he was called to go out into a place which he should after receive for an inheritance, obeyed; and he went out, not knowing whither he went... for he looked for a city which hath foundations, whose builder and maker is God"* (Heb. 11:8,10). Abraham was willing to let go of everything that had been familiar to him. He left his home, his relatives, and even his own country to find the place to which God had called him. Revelation provides spiritual sight and the secret of Abraham is found in the simple fact that he obeyed what he had seen. When Abraham was called by God, there was nothing special with him. He was not known for his righteous lifestyle or extraordinary deeds. Abraham was an ordinary, idol-worshipping gentile that God had chosen by grace. Abraham's life story became special because he responded to the calling of God by faith (Gen. 11:27-12:4).

Abraham was looking for the city of God, and he carried a clear vision of this city in his spirit. This vision gave him strength and endurance to persevere through the challenging journey to find this city. In the spirit, Abraham had seen the glory of the New Jerusalem and the day of the New Covenant that came through Jesus Christ. *"Your father Abraham rejoiced to see my day: and he saw it, and was glad" (John 8:56).* This gave Abraham the strength and courage that he needed to move on with God.

### Our Journey into the City of God

Our journey has many similarities to the journey of Abraham. When we have seen the glory of the New Jerusalem, we can no longer stay in that old familiar place of religion. Instead, we will be compelled to go on a journey with the Father. This journey will take us through unknown and unfamiliar territory, but the goal of the journey is glorious. The New Jerusalem is the body of Christ in all its beauty and grace. We were created for intimacy with our heavenly Bridegroom and beholding Him will ruin our appetite for religion. Only the true life that is found in our union with Jesus Christ can satisfy our soul. The places where we find His life and expressions of divine love, are places where the heavenly city has been established.

**Activations**

- Set aside 20-30 minutes for prayer. Ask the Holy Spirit to reveal what it means for us to be the New Jerusalem. Read through the list of New Creation realities that we found by studying the Holy City earlier in this chapter. Read it slowly while asking the Holy Spirit to highlight two or three of the points on this list. Invite Him to give you deeper insight into the New Jerusalem. Write down the revelations that you receive.

- The New Jerusalem came down from heaven to steward the glory of God here in this world. This is our mission! Ask Him to make you a wise steward of the glory of God that reveals the heart of Jesus everywhere.

- The book of Revelation describes two different cities, the New Jerusalem and Babylon. These two cities represent two contrasting spiritual realities. The New Jerusalem is the bride of the Lamb, while Babylon is the great harlot, the religious spirit. Read about these two cities in the book of Revelation and ask the Holy Spirit for more light on the spiritual realities they represent.

- Take time in prayer to ask Jesus to reveal if Babylon has influenced you in any way and ask Him to deliver you from any stronghold of religion. Ask Him to fill your life with the realities of the New Jerusalem.

# CHAPTER 6: UNITED WITH JESUS

For us to access all the blessings of our bridal identity, we need to understand what it means to be united with Jesus Christ. There is nothing as liberating and empowering as knowing that we are in Him. Another way of saying that we have been united with Jesus is to say that we are in Christ. We are one with Jesus and as He is, so are we in this world (1 John 4:17).

Knowing who I am in Christ has changed my life forever. In the early years of being a believer, my passion was to live in intimacy with Jesus in total alignment with His heart. But at that time, I did not understand what it meant to be in Christ. When I first heard teaching on this topic, it felt a bit confusing. I had been used to think of my relationship with Jesus in terms of following Him, seeking after Him, or being a God chaser. I struggled for some time to grasp this language of union and "being in Christ", but as I understood that I am united with Christ, I entered a rest of faith that I had not experienced before. Knowing who I am in Christ defines my identity as a son and it gives me boldness in my relationship with the Father.

## What Does It Mean to Be in Christ?

We have received a new identity in Christ, which means that we are no longer defined by our past experiences, neither good nor bad ones. Other people's opinions of us should never be allowed to shape our identity, not even our own opinions. The only thing that matters is that we are a new creation in Christ. *"Therefore if any man be in Christ, he is a new creature: old things are passed away; behold, all things are become new"* (2 Cor. 5:17). To be in Christ simply means that everything that is true about Him, is now true about us as well. Jesus became like us, so that we might become as He is (2 Cor. 5:21). We are now as righteous and holy as Jesus is. This does not describe some vague spiritual position, but these new creation realities reveal our true identity.

## My Journey of Healing

Receiving inner healing and restoration is all about learning to see ourselves through the Father's eyes. Encountering His love will deliver us from destructive thinking and set us free from the pain of the past. The Father loves us the way we are, but He loves us too much to leave us in that state. The good news is that Jesus has already provided our healing and restoration through the cross. As you keep on reading this book, you'll notice that getting to know the heart of Jesus Christ has been a journey of healing and restoration for me. Two things have been very important for me throughout this journey:

- *The vision of a healed and restored life.* As the Holy Spirit showed me that the Father's plan for me was to be transformed into Christlikeness, and when I started to grasp what that would look like, I found hope. There are no bondages or wounds in Jesus. He lives in a total peace and complete wholeness and freedom. Since this is true about Jesus, I realized that this was His plan for me as well. I started to dream of a life of wholeness and peace. That gave me hope and vision of a restored life.

- *Knowing who I am in Christ.* As I embraced my new identity in a deeper way, I saw how inner healing flows from knowing who I am in Christ. Healing is not about chasing after new breakthroughs and deeper cleansing. It is about resting in the finished work of Jesus Christ. Healing has already been given to us (Isa. 53:4-5).

A lot of believers are striving to find healing and freedom. They are being stressed out by the pressure of chasing breakthroughs in healing and deliverance. Since they are not finding what they are looking for, they feel like they have missed out on God's will. That leaves them stuck in disappointment and condemnation. When a believer doesn't know his or her identity in Christ, there is no foundation for their faith to rest on. That leaves them in a hard place where they must trust in their own works. But our identity in Christ provides a secure foundation because Jesus will never change. Since Jesus remains the same, our identity is secure, even while we are going through a process of healing and restoration.

## As Jesus Is, So Are We

The key to understand the concept of being in Christ is to know about the law of identification. When Jesus went to the cross, He became like us, so that He could make us as He is (1 John 4:17). This is the reason that Paul could say that Jesus became sin, to make us the righteousness of God in Him (2 Cor. 5:21). Jesus was made a curse for us, so that we could be blessed and filled with the Holy Spirit. *"Christ hath redeemed us from the curse of the law, being made a curse for us: for it is written, cursed is every one that hangeth on a tree: that the blessing of Abraham might come on the Gentiles through Jesus Christ; that we might receive the promise of the Spirit through faith" (Gal. 3:13-14).* We can trust the finished work of Christ and let the love of the Father define us. This is possible because we are now united with Him and share His life.

## We Are in Union with Jesus

Being in Christ is to be united with Jesus, which means that our identity and our inheritance are kept safe in Him. Since Jesus carries the government of the Kingdom of God on His shoulders,

He is doing all the hard work. We reap all the benefits of that because we are in Him. Isaiah makes the following declaration about Jesus: *"For unto us a child is born, unto us a son is given: and the government shall be upon his shoulder: and his name shall be called Wonderful, Counsellor, The mighty God, The everlasting Father, The Prince of Peace. Of the increase of his government and peace there shall be no end" (Isa. 9:6-7)*. Because of our union with Jesus Christ, our inheritance and destiny rest on His shoulders, and we live in the increase of peace and government that He brings.

### Receiving Life as a Gift

When life has been filled with pain and brokenness, it is easy to develop a very negative and cynical approach to life, viewing it as something that we must endure until we get to heaven. As we are being healed, our view of being alive will change so that we can receive life as a blessing. We are then set free to enjoy our life as the gift that it truly is. Our union with Jesus Christ is not made a reality through a lifelong program of asceticism. Even though we are called to live a life of sanctification, our focus should not be on dying to sin. Through Christ, our old life *has* been crucified, we *have* died and we *have* been raised to a new life (Gal. 2:19-20). The life we have in Jesus is a wonderful gift, full of the creativity and wonders of heaven.

### We Have Been Made Alive

*"For the death that He died, He died to sin once for all; but the life that He lives, He lives to God. Likewise you also, reckon yourselves to be dead indeed to sin, but alive to God in Christ Jesus our Lord" (Rom. 6:10-11 NKJV)*. We have died from the power of sin and have been made alive unto God through our union with Jesus. This revelation kills religion because legalistic teachings are always steeped in sin consciousness. Since we have died to sin, there is

no need to focus on it. Our focus should be on living the new life that is ours in Christ. Our heavenly Father has blessed us with a life of endless possibilities, making it possible for us to enjoy our inheritance as His children to the fullest.

### Crucified, Dead & Resurrected

As we have already seen, to understand how we have been made alive through Jesus, we need to have a revelation on the law of identification. Jesus not only died for us. He died *as* us, making us one with Him in His death. Paul writes:

*For if we have become united with Him in the likeness of His death, certainly we shall also be in the likeness of His resurrection, knowing this, that our old self was crucified with Him, in order that our body of sin might be done away with, so that we would no longer be slaves to sin; for the one who has died is freed from sin (Rom. 6:5-7 NASB).*

When we died with Jesus, our old life was crucified and killed off. We died to sin, and we are now delivered from its power and influence. As a result, we have been united with Jesus Christ in His resurrection and share in His life with the Father. This is the meaning of being united with Him in marriage. *"Now if we have died with Christ, we believe that we shall also live with Him, knowing that Christ, having been raised from the dead, is never to die again; death no longer is master over Him. For the death that He died, He died to sin once for all time; but the life that He lives, He lives to God" (Rom. 6:8-10 NASB).* In the same way that Jesus is alive unto God, so we have been made alive to God. We can embrace the abundant life that Jesus came to give us.

## Abundant & Overflowing Life

Jesus came with a mission to give us life in its fullness until we overflow. Jesus Himself is abundance by nature, and He always gives everything out of His abundance. He is the Good Shepherd who laid down His life for us, to give us the life that the Father always planned for His children to have. God loves life and Jesus gave His life for us to make us fully alive.

*A thief has only one thing in mind—he wants to steal, slaughter, and destroy. But I have come to give you everything in abundance, more than you expect —life in its fullness until you overflow! I am the Good Shepherd who lays down my life as a sacrifice for the sheep (John 10:10-11 TPT).*

The devil wants to kill, steal and destroy. He wants to steal our lives, ruin our peace, and kill the joy of life, which is the reason that he invented religion. Religious teachings are always built on the lie that God is a stingy ruler who does not want us to enjoy life. That assumption is mistaken. The reality is that true life can only be found in Jesus.

## Jesus Brings Life!

One of the themes that runs throughout the whole Bible, is that Jesus Christ is our life. When He shows up, He brings life with Him. *"And this is the record, that God hath given to us eternal life, and this life is in his Son. He that hath the Son hath life; and he that hath not the Son of God hath not life"* (1 John 5:11-12). Wherever the power of Jesus Christ operates, the life of the Father is revealed. When a person receives Jesus, that person is made alive. It is by receiving the life of Jesus Christ that we have been saved. *"For if while we were enemies we were reconciled to God through the death of His Son, much more, having been reconciled, we shall be saved by His life" (Rom 5:10 NASB)*. Jesus is the most exciting and dynamic person in the universe, and to live with Him turns life into an adventure that never ends.

### Feasting on the Finished Work of Jesus Christ

Jesus speaks of the Kingdom of God as a party. In the parable of the lost son, the Kingdom of God is depicted as a celebration of the lost son coming home (Luke 15:11-32). As the son returned, the loving Father slaughtered the fattened calf, and threw a big party for his son, with a lot of feasting, singing, and dancing. This is the nature of the Kingdom of God. It is an eternal party, where we are feasting on the finished work of the cross: *"Then the angel said to me, "Write these words: Wonderfully blessed are those who are invited to feast at the wedding celebration of the Lamb" (Rev. 19:6-9 TPT)!* We have already been united with Jesus and the Father's full inheritance now belongs to us. We are invited to celebrate the finished work of Jesus every day. We live in the eternal party of being united with Christ, enjoying all the blessings that are ours in the New Covenant. We celebrate the victory of Jesus and we enjoy the rich dishes of His finished work on the cross. This is the abundant life that we have received through Jesus Christ.

### Crucified with Christ

Because we have been crucified with Christ we have died to the power of sin and therefore the world no longer has any authority over us. *"I am crucified with Christ: nevertheless I live; yet not I, but Christ liveth in me: and the life which I now live in the flesh I live by the faith of the Son of God, who loved me, and gave himself for me" (Gal. 2:20).* We have received the abundant life in Christ and as that life overflows within our hearts it will transform the world around us. Jesus Christ indwells us and He wants to live His life through us. His power is greater than the powers of this world.

We have overcome the world together with Him (1 John 4:4). This is the reason that we can live in the world and yet not be living with the world as our source. When Jesus came into our hearts, He brought the life of God with Him. As we are walking with Jesus, His life will transform dead and broken areas of our soul. Let's allow the Holy Spirit to minister healing to our hearts so that we can be fully alive, flowing in the creativity and wisdom of heaven to release the life of Christ everywhere!

## Activations

- Set aside 20-30 minutes for prayer. Ask the Holy Spirit to give deeper insight into your union with Jesus Christ. Invite Him to reveal how this revelation changes your relationship with God. Write down what He reveals.

- Since all of us struggle with some brokenness, we need more healing and restoration. How does the revelation of being united with Jesus help us to receive healing and restoration? Invite the Holy Spirit to give more insight on this topic. Ask Jesus to minister healing to the broken areas in your life.

- The law of identification means that Jesus became as we are, so that we could become as He is. Knowing this will change our lives in a radical way. Invite the Holy Spirit to highlight at least three areas of your life that need to be transformed in light of this revelation. Invite Jesus to minister to you in these areas.

- Jesus came to give you abundant life. Ask Him to show you what that life looks like. Then ask Him to fill you with that life until it overflows so that you can minister the life of Christ wherever you are.

# CHAPTER 7: TREASURES FROM THE SONG OF SONGS

One of the most powerful portraits of our union with Christ is found in the Song of Solomon. This truly is the song of all songs, the most beautiful love song ever written.  It unveils the romance of the ages. This song speaks beautifully of the burning love of Jesus Christ and the passionate response of His beloved bride. The amount of revelation contained within this poem is so vast that it could fill many books. Here we are going to look at some of the treasures hidden within the Song of Solomon that reveals the love of Jesus for His bride. We are not going to walk through the whole song, but we will look at some of the passages that reveal the love of Jesus Christ.

## A Seal upon His Heart

We know that Jesus lives within our heart, but He carries us in His heart as well. Jesus adores us so much that he placed us as a seal upon His heart and on His arm:

*"Place me like a seal over your heart, like a seal on your arm; for love is as strong as death, its jealousy unyielding as the grave. It burns like blazing fire, like a mighty flame. Many waters cannot quench love; rivers cannot sweep it away. If one were to give all the wealth of one's house for love, it would be utterly scorned"* (Song. 8:6-7 NIV).

We are passionate for what God is doing, which is a beautiful thing. But our passion for Him is nothing when compared to His burning passion for us. Jesus loves us and He longs to spend time with us so that He can reveal His beauty and glory to us. There is so much comfort and healing to be found in knowing that we are always in the heart of our Bridegroom.

## The Beauty of Jesus

The Song of songs begins with the bride singing a song of love and adoration to Jesus Christ. This is where it all starts. When we behold Jesus as He truly is, our hearts will be captivated by His beauty. The bride loves Jesus deeply and asks for His kisses. She wants to be close to Him. Jesus wants to shower us with kisses, but He will not do it unless we invite Him. *"May he kiss me with the kisses of his mouth! For your love is sweeter than wine. "Your oils have a pleasing fragrance, your name is like purified oil; therefore the young women love you. "Draw me after you and let's run together! The king has brought me into his chambers" (Song 1:2-4 NASB).* Jesus is the anointed one, and His presence brings the pleasant fragrance of pure life (2 Cor. 2:15-16). Being kissed with the kisses of His mouth speaks of the infilling of the Holy Spirit, whose presence sets our hearts ablaze and immerses us in the love of Christ.

The name of Jesus is like an oil poured out, and when we speak His name, the sick is healed, the angels sing and the powers of darkness tremble. Jesus has brought us into the bridal chamber, where we abide in an unbreakable union with Him. No one can enter this secret place except Jesus and His bride. There we can contemplate His beauty and abide in His love. Our Bridegroom is not silent when He hears our worship and adoration.

Jesus passionately responds to the bride: *"My darling, you are so lovely! You are beauty itself to me. Your passionate eyes are like gentle doves" (Song 1:15 TPT).* Jesus is the eternal Word of God, and His words brings restoration, freedom and healing. There are many ways to receive healing from God, but one of the most powerful ways in which we'll find restoration, is by listening to His voice as He speaks words of love into our heart. If we want to hear what Jesus is speaking, we need to shut out the other voices that want to pull our hearts away from Him.

## The Distracting Voices of Religion

The voices of religion want to steal our attention away from our Bridegroom. Most of the time, these voices belong to believers who lack a revelation of the New Covenant and our union with Christ. This makes them blind to the value of a life of rest and intimacy with Jesus. They think that we are wasting our gifts and calling by building a lifestyle of intimacy with Jesus in the secret place. These voices are fueled by guilt and condemnation. They want to convince us to join them and become caretakers of their vineyards. This is a picture of forsaking the bridal chamber for religious work and ministry:

*"My mother's sons were angry with me; They made me caretaker of the vineyards, But I have not taken care of my own vineyard. "Tell me, you whom my soul loves, Where do you pasture your flock, Where do you have it lie down at noon? For why should I be like one who veils herself beside the flocks of your companions" (Song 1:6-7 NASB).*

This passage shows us what will happen when the bride listens to the distracting voices coming from religion. As she abandoned her vineyard of intimacy, she left her fellowship with Jesus in order to fulfill religious obligations. That left her frustrated and distressed. Eventually, she realized that the vineyard of her heart had been left untended and that her precious fellowship with the Bridegroom was lost.

## Returning to Intimacy with Jesus

When working for God distracts us from living in intimacy with Jesus by causing us to become more concerned with our vision than tending to our vineyard of intimacy, then our work for God has become an idol. When that happens, we need to slow down and regain our focus on Jesus by tending the garden of our heart.

As we turn back to intimacy with Jesus, it might feel as though we have lost our fellowship with Him, that He is now distant and cannot be found (Song 1:7). But that is never the case. Jesus is always there for us and we can easily reconnect with Him by turning our eyes back to Him.

*Listen, my radiant one— if you ever lose sight of me, just follow in my footsteps where I lead my lovers. Come with your burdens and cares. Come to the place near the sanctuary of my shepherds. My dearest one, let me tell you how I see you— you are so thrilling to me (Song 1:8-9 TPT).*

Jesus wants our full attention when we become distracted by ministry or through religious activities. He calls us back to Himself. As we return to Jesus, He will remind us of our identity. Religion is only attractive to the person who have forgot their true identity. Jesus wants to rescue us from religious labor by drawing us back into a place of intimacy and rest. Working for God becomes empty if we forsake a lifestyle of intimacy.

I have learned to live with this tension in my life with Jesus. I love to preach, write and to be involved in missions. But I love intimacy with God even more, so I have made sure that my first hours of the day are spent in fellowship with the Father, Jesus and the Holy Spirit. I want everything to come as a fruit of my relationship with God. Ministry is meant to be an expression of our inner life of fellowship with Jesus Christ.

### Catching the Little Foxes

The song of Solomon depicts these distractions as little foxes that ruin our vineyard by distracting us from our union with Jesus. Solomon writes:

*You must catch the troubling foxes, those sly little foxes that hinder our relationship. For they raid our budding vineyard of love to ruin what I've planted within you. Will you catch them and remove them for me? We will do it together (Song 2:15 TPT).*

Usually, we are not distracted by the one big thing or situation in life. It is the many small things when put together tend to steal our attention. These distractions can create a lifestyle where we spend very little time in the secret place with Jesus. Fortunately, Jesus is good at hunting these little foxes, and He will catch and kill them for us as soon as we ask for His help. When we realize that we have become distracted and too busy with life, there is no condemnation for us (Rom. 8:1). We just need to allow Him to refocus our attention on Him.

## The Watchmen of Religion

Some of the religious brothers are not satisfied by just overseeing the vineyards of legalism. These dear brothers have evolved into becoming watchmen that are attacking and hurting the bride, while she seeks deeper intimacy with Jesus. *"The watchmen who make the rounds in the city found me, they struck me and wounded me; the guards of the walls took my shawl away from me. "Swear to me, you daughters of Jerusalem, if you find my beloved, as to what you will tell him: For I am lovesick" (Song 4:7-8 NASB).* These self-appointed guardians of the Kingdom of God want to control the bride. They do this because of fear and pride and their ministry harms the bride of Christ. Their advice and their so-called wisdom damage her soul because they lack revelation of the New Covenant.
Instead, they are using the law, guarding the walls and the gates of the city to make sure that no one goes too far into the fields of grace and intimacy with Jesus. The bride doesn't give up though but keeps looking for her Bridegroom.

We have all met these watchmen at times. They value balance over radical love for Jesus, and they prefer religious appearance over a heart of brokenness and humility because they don't know the heart of the Father. Their advice is filled with legalism and their teaching is built on religious thinking and traditions. If we have been damaged by religious ministries, Jesus wants to bring healing and restoration. He wants to heal the wounds caused by religion by bringing us through a deep process of restoration. The most important thing is that we don't give up but keep going further in fellowship and intimacy with Jesus. With Him we will find true life and freedom, and the Holy Spirit will lead us into fruitfulness and blessing.

**Jesus Ministers New Wine to Refresh Our Hearts**

Those who have suffered under the oppression of religion and legalism must realize that we will never find healing or favor by getting stuck in disappointment and bitterness. Jesus heals us by bringing us into His house of wine.

*Suddenly, he transported me into his house of wine— he looked upon me with his unrelenting love divine. Revive me with your raisin cakes. Refresh me again with your apples. Help me and hold me, for I am lovesick! I am longing for more— yet how could I take more? His left hand cradles my head while his right hand holds me close. I am at rest in this love (Song 2:4-6 TPT).*

Jesus fills our cup with the finest wine of His grace, causing our hearts to be revived by revelation. At His table we are refreshed by feasting on the fruit of the Spirit. In His embrace, we find healing and restoration from the wounds of religion. We find rest in His love. Jesus is the true Vine, and the wine that He provides refreshes the broken soul. *"And the vine said unto them, Should I leave my wine, which cheereth God and man, and go to be promoted over the trees" (Judg. 9:13)?* When we have been wounded and left disillusioned by religion, drinking the wine of the New Covenant will cheer us up again!

## Coming Out of the Desert, Leaning on the Beloved

Sooner or later, we will experience seasons of dryness where our spiritual life feels more like a dry desert than the garden of Eden. Some people have even constructed a theology out of wilderness experiences. But Jesus does not want us to get stuck there. His only goal when we are stuck in a dry season is to bring us out of the wilderness: *"I charge you, O daughters of Jerusalem, that ye stir not up, nor awake my love, until he please. Who is this that cometh up from the wilderness, Leaning upon her beloved" (Song 8:4-5).* During seasons of spiritual drought, many people become self-centered, wondering what they have done wrong. That will not help. We can't get out of the wilderness by ourselves. Only Jesus can help us with that. He goes into the wilderness to find us and lead us out. As we lean on Him, He brings us out of the desert and into a place of fruitfulness. *"Who is this that cometh out of the wilderness like pillars of smoke, perfumed with myrrh and frankincense, with all powders of the merchant" (Song 3:6)?* Jesus only knows of a coming-out-of the desert theology.

Because Jesus indwells us, rivers of living water flow out of our innermost being, which means that we have been delivered from seasons of spiritual drought (John 7:37-38). When Jesus went into the wilderness to be tempted by Satan, He did not bring any of the disciples. Jesus went there alone as our substitute to break the cycle of the dry seasons in the spirit, so that we can live in an eternal season of fruitfulness. If you are still stuck in a wilderness experience, remember that Jesus is coming for you. He will not leave you in a place of dryness and barrenness. Jesus makes you fruitful by leading you to still waters and green pastures where you will find rest for your soul (Ps. 23:1-2). Lean on Jesus and let Him bring you into the land of blessing and freedom.

## He Comes Jumping Over the Mountains

Even though religion tries to distract us by the voices of angry siblings and legalistic watchmen, we don't have to lose our focus on Jesus. Satan raises mountains of religion and hills of legalism to hinder us, but his activities cannot stop Jesus from pursuing us. He has the feet of a hind and the strength of a young stag. He jumps over these mountain tops, leaping over the hills with ease. Jesus is walking right through the walls of legalism to reach our hearts and to shower us with love and mercy. *"Listen! My beloved! Behold, he comes, climbing on the mountains, leaping and running on the hills! My beloved is like a gazelle or a young stag. He is looking through the windows, He is gazing through the lattice"* (Song 2:8-9 NASB).

## Jesus is Our Breakthrough

When we abide in Jesus, we can access that same grace to leap over the mountains and walk through walls. Being in union with Christ is our guarantee of victory. We have been made more than conquerors through Him who loves us (Rom. 8:37). As we abide in His presence, we'll find strength to jump over the mountains with feet like the hinds. I have seen this time and time again in my life. When I am going through a spiritual battle, I overcome through intimacy with Jesus. In His presence, there is always renewal and new life. Jesus Himself is our breakthrough and He gives strength to endure, even if we are going through some challenging seasons. Sometimes, we walk in victory by speaking to the mountains (Mark 11:22-24). At other times, we receive the grace from God to jump over the mountains on the feet of hinds (Hab. 3:17-19). We need to allow Jesus to lead us forward as He chooses to. The important thing is to know that Jesus Himself is the big Breaker that provides grace and strength to overcome through His love.

## The New Covenant of Singing and Fruitfulness

Jesus has brought us out of the Old Covenant, where we had to endure the harsh winter of barrenness, and where the cold rain of legalism quenched our passion for Jesus. Our Bridegroom has now brought us into the New Covenant. We live in the summer of fruitfulness under the sun of righteousness that has risen with healing in its wings (Mal. 4:2).

*Arise, my darling, my beautiful one, come with me. See! The winter is past; the rains are over and gone. Flowers appear on the earth; the season of singing has come, the cooing of doves is heard in our land. The fig tree forms its early fruit; the blossoming vines spread their fragrance. Arise, come, my darling; my beautiful one, come with me (Song 2:10-13 NIV).*

This is the season of singing, where the voice of the turtledove is being heard all over the land. Just like the Holy Spirit descended like a dove upon Jesus, His gentle presence has now descended upon us, and we can hear Him singing a song of adoration, which unveils the beauty of Christ. We are living in an eternal season of fruitfulness where we are enjoying the song of the Holy Spirit, who sings the love song of Jesus and His bride. The New Covenant is not a covenant of obeying the letter of the law, but it operates by the anointing and empowering presence of the Holy Spirit (2 Cor. 3:6).

## Do Not Disturb Love

We have been invited to find rest and peace in the love of Christ. We have seen how Satan tries to disturb our rest through religion and by the distractions of life. Jesus addresses these distractions several times within the Song of Songs: *"Daughters of Jerusalem, I charge you by the gazelles and by the does of the field: Do no  arouse or awaken love until it so desires." (Song 3:5, 2:7, 8:4 NIV).* No matter what these voices are speaking, we don't have to allow them to steal our rest in Christ. Jesus is our life, and we find our purpose and fulfillment in being loved by Him. As we listen to His voice, we will hear him speak words of life over us that unveils how we have been perfected in Christ.

## Jesus Speaks to Affirm Our Bridal Identity

Whatever is going on in our lives, we can be certain that Jesus loves us and knows who we really are. In the Song of Solomon, Jesus is speaking His words of love and grace over us, affirming our identity as His beautiful, beloved, and spotless bride. These words are for us today:

- *When we think that we are unworthy, Jesus responds by declaring how lovely we are to Him.* *"Jerusalem maidens, in this twilight darkness I know I am so unworthy—so in need. Yet you are so lovely" (Song 1:5 TPT)!*

- *When we feel dry and our lives looks like a wilderness or a wasteland, Jesus sees us as His beloved and holy bride.* *"I feel as dark and dry as the desert tents of the wandering nomads. Yet you are so lovely— like the fine linen tapestry hanging in the Holy Place" (Song 1:5 TPT).*

- ***When we are surrounded by enemies, having been wounded by the spiritual battle, Jesus declares that we are pure as a lily.*** *"Yes, you are my darling companion. You stand out from all the rest. For though the thorns surround you, you remain as pure as a lily, more than all others" (Song 2:2 TPT).*

- ***When we feel weak and insecure, Jesus speaks strength and security into our hearts.*** *"When I look at you, I see your inner strength, so stately and strong. You are as secure as David's fortress. Your virtues and grace cause a thousand famous soldiers to surrender to your beauty. Your pure faith and love rest over your heart as you nurture those who are yet infants" (Song. 4:4-5 TPT).*

- ***When we feel vulnerable and unprotected, Jesus speaks protection and growth into us.*** *"But now I have grown and become a bride, and my love for him has made me a tower of passion and contentment for my beloved. I am now a firm wall of protection for others, guarding them from harm. This is how he sees me—I am the one who brings him bliss, finding favor in his eyes" (Song. 8:9-10 TPT).*

- ***When we feel barren and our lives seems to lack fruit, Jesus speaks a change of season and declares fruitfulness into our heart.*** *"The season has changed, the bondage of your barren winter has ended, and the season of hiding is over and gone. The rains have soaked the earth and left it bright with blossoming flowers. The season for singing and pruning the vines has arrived. I hear the cooing of doves in our land, filling the air with songs to awaken you and guide you forth" (Song 2:11-12 TPT).*

- ***When we feel that we have lost our voice, Jesus reveals that our words are full of mercy and grace. Our words refresh the weary and brings pleasure to Jesus.*** *"Your lips are as lovely as Rahab's scarlet ribbon, speaking mercy, speaking grace. The words of your mouth are as refreshing as an oasis. What pleasure you bring to me" (Song 4:3 TPT)!*

- ***When we feel like our worship is empty, Jesus tells us that our praise releases milk and honey and that the fragrance of our worship is lovely.*** *Your loving words are like the honeycomb to me; your tongue releases milk and honey, for I find the promised land flowing within you. The fragrance of your worshiping love surrounds you with scented robes of white" (Song 4:11 TPT).*

- ***When we feel that we are damaged and beyond hope of restoration because of our past, Jesus calls us radiant and beautiful.*** *"Arise, my dearest. Hurry, my darling. Come away with me! I have come as you have asked to draw you to my heart and lead you out. For now is the time, my beautiful one" (Song 2:10 TPT).*

- ***When we feel like our life is empty and that we have lost our fire, Jesus calls us fruitful and sees a wellspring of living water flowing out of our belly.*** *"Your inward life is now sprouting, bringing forth fruit. What a beautiful paradise unfolds within you. When I'm near you, I smell aromas of the finest spice, for many clusters of my exquisite fruit now grow within your inner garden… You are a fountain of gardens. A well of living water springs up from within you, like a mountain brook flowing into my heart" (Song 4:13, 15 TPT).*

No matter what we are going through, Jesus sees who we really are. He is always speaking words of encouragement and comfort to establish us in our identity. He keeps on pursuing us by calling us back into His presence. There we are being transformed, until our false identities have been consumed by the flames of His love. This revelation has changed my life in a dramatic way. All my life, I had been listening to many destructive voices that had told me that I was a failure. Only Jesus could penetrate the lairs of lies that surrounded my heart and call me back to life.

- Read the Song of Songs together with Jesus. Listen to His voice speak to you through this song, calling you into the chambers of intimacy with Him. Ask the Holy Spirit to reveal your identity as His beloved bride while you are reading. Repeat this activation a couple of times and write down what Jesus speaks to you.

- Set aside 20-30 minutes for prayer. Ask the Holy Spirit to expose and catch the little foxes that steal your focus from Jesus. There might be things in your life that makes it hard for you to stay focused on Him. Invite the Holy Spirit to refocus your attention back unto Jesus.

- Like most believers, you have probably been wounded and influenced by religion at some point. Invite Jesus to heal your heart from the wounds of religion and deliver you from all legalism in your life.

- Go back and read the list of identity statements that Jesus speaks over you from the Song of Songs. Then ask the Holy Spirit to highlight some of the statements in it. Ask Him to give you more revelation on your identity and invite Him to minister to your heart in the areas that He shows you.

# CHAPTER 8: THE JEALOUS LOVE OF JESUS CHRIST

We have already seen that our God is a consuming fire, who is jealous for us. Jesus wants our hearts to be set solely on Him. *"For the LORD thy God is a consuming fire, even a jealous God"* (Deut. 4:24). Many people associate jealousy with fear or control. That's what human jealousy usually looks like, but the jealousy of God is different. His jealousy is rooted in His sacrificial love for us. The Father knows the damage that idolatry and a divided heart will cause. Idolatry is such a serious matter to God because it steals our hearts away from Christ. To worship idols is spiritual adultery, which severely harms our relationship with Jesus. This is what caused the apostle Paul to be filled with godly jealousy, making it His goal to present a pure and fully devoted virgin to Christ: *"For I am jealous for you with a godly jealousy; for I betrothed you to one husband, to present you as a pure virgin to Christ. But I am afraid that, as the serpent deceived Eve by his trickery, your minds will be led astray from sincere and pure devotion to Christ"* (2 Cor. 11:2-3 *NASB*).

When we grow in our revelation of Jesus as our Bridegroom, our hearts will continually be filled with a purer devotion to Him. Jesus longs for a deeper intimacy with us and He passionately hates everything that could harm His bride. Idolatry is one of the worst transgressions there is. It was because of idolatry that the people of Israel were exiled from the promised land. It is still idolatry that hinders us from living in a deeper relationship with Jesus today.

### Idols Are False Lovers

An idol is really a demonic power in disguise, and committing idolatry is to give honor and worship to these demons. The Old

Testament prophets speak of false gods in terms of illegitimate spiritual lovers and they equal this kind of false worship with spiritual adultery (Jer. 4:30, 22:20-22, Ezek. 16:36-37, 23). Behind idols like Baal and the Asherim, there were demons at work. These demonic powers did miracles and performed supernatural signs to seduce the people of God to worshipping false gods. The Bible condemns idolatry in strong words but we must remember that the reason that God addressed idolatry with such passion is rooted in His deep love for us. The Father knows that the powers behind these idols are demonic powers that want to deceive His children into bondage and death.

### Committing Spiritual Adultery with the Law

It is important to remember that the Word of God speaks of being united to Christ as a marriage, but it describes our relationship to the law in terms of marriage as well:

*So, my dear brothers and sisters, the same principle applies to your relationship with God. For you died to your first husband, the law, by being co-crucified with the body of the Messiah. So you are now free to "marry" another—the one who was raised from the dead so that you may now bear spiritual fruit for God (Rom 7:4 TPT).*

Since we have died to our marriage with the law through the redemptive work of Jesus, our relationship to the law has ended completely. We have neither obligation, nor any need, to relate to the law whatsoever. We are now married to Jesus and have been united with Him forever. Going back under the law for guidance in our relationship with God, or using it for spiritual growth, is both idolatry and unfaithfulness to Christ! This might sound extreme but think about it. What would it be called if I stayed for the night with an old girlfriend, even though I am now married to Linda? That is called adultery. In the same way, for the believer to go back under the law is unfaithfulness to Christ. This happens when we fall into legalism, thinking that we can be more pleasing to God through our good works.

## The Accuser Needs the Law to Oppress Us

When a believer accepts a legalistic belief system, he or she is in a sense re-arming a disarmed devil, by giving back his weapons. Since Satan is the accuser of the brethren, his main weapon is the law. The devil is defeated because Jesus took the punishment for our sins and thereby closed every case against us. That has made the devil's weapons useless. Satan was using the law to accuse us and before the cross he had a legal right to do so, because of our sins. But now our sins are forgiven, and all accusations have been invalidated and are therefore irrelevant. *"He canceled the record of the charges against us and took it away by nailing it to the cross. In this way, he disarmed the spiritual rulers and authorities. He shamed them publicly by his victory over them on the cross"* (Col. 2:14-15 NLT). Satan is not only an accuser, but a deceiver and liar as well (John 8:44). He doesn't play fair. He knows that he no longer has the right to accuse us, but he doesn't want us to know that. If we go back under the law, we will open the door for him to use legalism and accusation to put us back under condemnation and religious oppression.

## Appearing as an Angel of Light

We started this chapter by reading from 2 Corinthians 11. We are now going back there to expose Satan's most successful strategy when it comes to deceiving the bride of Christ away from the simple gospel: *"And no marvel; for Satan himself is transformed into an angel of light. Therefore it is no great thing if his ministers also be transformed as the ministers of righteousness; whose end shall be according to their works"* (2 Cor. 11:14-15).

If Satan would appear like an ugly snake or a dragon to tempt us, we would expose his deceptions immediately. Therefore, he masks himself as an angel of light instead, appearing as a servant of righteousness by trying to sound like the Holy Spirit. Satan tells us that we are saved by Jesus and that the New Covenant is wonderful… but not enough. He then continues by suggesting that we need to add our own works to the cross for us to grow spiritually. He wants us to believe that we need Jesus Christ plus something more. But if we add something to the all-sufficiency of Jesus Christ, we will make the gospel void of power in our lives.

My previous book, *Partnering with the Love of Christ*, explored the theme of spiritual disciplines from a New Covenant perspective. I was a bit hesitant to write that book at first, because I didn't want people to misunderstand what I tried to communicate. My fear was that some of my readers might end up assuming that we need to perform these spiritual disciplines to please God, but that is not the case at all. Partnering with Jesus means responding to His love so that the Kingdom of God can manifest through us.

## The Danger of Mixture

Just like the bride of Christ is depicted as the New Jerusalem in the book of Revelation, the religious spirit is described as the great harlot and the great city of Babylon (Rev. 17-18, 21:2,9-11). As we saw earlier, Babylon means *confusion* or *mixture*. This means that if we mix grace and law, we will end up in confusion. Mixing law and grace limits us from cultivating intimacy with Christ and from enjoying the benefits of the New Covenant. Jesus wants us to enjoy our inheritance to the fullest, by feasting on all the royal dishes at the King's table. He hates religion because it robs us of our blessings and inheritance.

## The Reason for His Jealousy

This was the reason that Paul was worried that the Corinthians should be deceived away from the simplicity that is in Christ (2 Cor. 11:3). Jesus does not want us to enter demonic territory. That will give Satan a legal right to oppress us and we know what will happen to the person who lives under his yoke of condemnation. *"The thief cometh not, but for to steal, and to kill, and to destroy: I am come that they might have life, and that they might have it more abundantly" (John 10:10).* Relating to the demonic realm will always lead to defeat. Jesus wants us to live an abundant life with Him. This is the reason for Him being so passionate in protecting us from every other spiritual power. Jesus knows that only by abiding in Him can we be fully satisfied. Religion appears like wisdom and those practicing it often has an aura of "holiness and humility" to them, but the fruit of legalism will be spiritual death and destruction. This is the reason that our Bridegroom burns with holy jealousy for us.

## The Idol of Legalism and Manmade Religion

We have received the abundant life from Jesus by grace through faith, and just as we received Jesus, we are to walk in Him. *"As ye have therefore received Christ Jesus the Lord, so walk ye in him: rooted and built up in him, and stablished in the faith, as ye have been taught, abounding therein with thanksgiving" (Col. 2:7).* As we learn to live out of our union with Christ, we will be built up and established in our new life. Therefore, whatever deceives us to put our trust in anything other than Jesus, is to be considered as idolatry that will ruin our life. Paul gives us a clear warning that is as relevant today as ever. *"Beware lest any man spoil you through philosophy and vain deceit, after the tradition of men, after the rudiments of the world, and not after Christ" (Col. 2:8).*

The biggest idol in the body of Christ today is legalism and the religious traditions of man. Jesus wants to deliver us from  these traditions, and especially the type of traditions that tries to buy God's favor through trading with good works.

**Jesus Cleanses the Temple**

Jesus showed a temper as He cleansed the temple by driving out the money changers and those who sold sacrificial animals there. This shows us that the Lion of Judah is not a tame lion and that He is very passionate for His own household. God is love and everything that Jesus did was motivated by love. We sometimes have a sentimental picture of the love of God, but His love can at times be very passionate and intense:

*And He entered the temple area and began to drive out those who were selling and buying on the temple grounds, and He overturned the tables of the money changers and the seats of those who were selling doves; and He would not allow anyone to carry merchandise through the temple grounds. And He began to teach and say to them, "Is it not written: 'My house will be called a house of prayer for all the nations'? But you have made it a den of robbers (Mark. 12:15-17 NASB).*

Jesus didn't cleanse the temple just because he had a bad day and lost His temper. Jesus performed a prophetic act here, pointing to the New Covenant. The New Covenant does not operate by trading with good works and it doesn't require our sacrifices. We have already received the fullness of God in Christ; the whole Kingdom belongs to us. In Christ, we receive everything as a gift of grace. Jesus drove out the moneychangers to make this point. There is no need for us to try to do business with God through good works. Jesus is burning with zeal for His bride and this prophetic act was a sign of His passionate love for us. *"And his disciples remembered that it was written, the zeal of thine house hath eaten me up" (John 2:17).* Jesus is still challenging religion with the same intense passion today, because He wants to drive out all legalism from our lives.

## Liberty in Christ

We saw earlier how the finished work of Jesus Christ silenced Satan's accusations and left him unemployed (Col.2:13-15). Paul continues his teaching on this topic by showing us how we have been set totally free from religion: *"So why would you allow anyone to judge you because of what you eat or drink, or insist that you keep the feasts, observe new moon celebrations, or the Sabbath? All of these were but a prophetic shadow and the evidence of what would be fulfilled, for the body is now Christ" (Col. 2:16-17 TPT)!* Because we are  in Christ, we should never allow religious standards or traditions to put us under condemnation. What we eat or drink, or whether we celebrate certain religious days has nothing to do with our standing with Christ. We could mention other spiritual practices here as well. They might help us but they have nothing to do with the believer's value in the Father's eyes.

The same principle applies to Old Testament practices. Knowing about the Old Testament feasts and customs can be very helpful because they are pointing to Christ. These are all shadows of the inheritance we have in Christ, but we need to understand that Jesus is the full manifestation of everything that the law pointed us to. *"Don't let anyone disqualify you from your prize! Don't let their pretended sincerity fool you as they deliberately lead you into their initiation of angel worship. For they take pleasure in pretending to be experts of something they know nothing about. Their reasoning is meaningless and comes only from their own opinion" (Col. 2:18 TPT).*

If we are not rooted and grounded in the love of Christ, we can easily end up disqualifying ourselves by coming under a yoke of religion, which always promotes the deception that Jesus is not enough for us. We have already seen how believing that Jesus is insufficient equals spiritual adultery. Our growth, righteousness and sanctification, all come from the head of the body, which is Jesus Himself: *"They refuse to take hold of the true source. But we receive directly from him, and his life supplies vitality into every part of his body through the joining ligaments connecting us all as one. He is the divine Head who guides his body and causes it to grow by the supernatural power of God"* (Col. 2:19 TPT).

### Refusing to Be Bullied by Religion

Paul continues by reminding us that we are dead to the religious systems and powers of this world. They are two sides of the same coin. Religion is just worldliness with God added into the mix. *"For you were included in the death of Christ and have died with him to the religious system and powers of this world. Don't retreat back to being bullied by the standards and opinions of religion"* (Col. 2:20 TPT). There is no reason for us to bow under religious pressure by allowing ourselves to be oppressed by religion and legalism. The religious spirit doesn't respect our freedom and boundaries, which means that legalism always has a forceful and controlling element to it. For this reason, God encourages us to stand firm in our freedom in Christ (Gal. 5:1). People get most confused when religion comes as a mixture of legalism and grace, which makes it important to know how to discern religion.

### The Characteristics of Religion

*"Don't retreat back to being bullied by the standards and opinions of religion—for example, their strict requirements, "You can't associate with that person!" or, "Don't eat that!" or, "You can't touch that!" These are the doctrines of men and corrupt customs that are worthless to help you spiritually"* (Col. 2:20-22 TPT)!

Paul mentions several characteristics of religion in this passage. Even though we are studying the "Christian" version of religion, these characteristics can be found in all religion.

The challenge is that intimacy with Jesus will sometimes appear very similar to a religious lifestyle. This is because our life with Christ is a matter of the heart. The difference is that the deeds of a living faith is an expression of our intimacy with Jesus, while religion is self-centered. I've put together a list that summarizes these characteristics, just to make clear what Paul is addressing:

- *"Their strict requirements"*. Religion always comes with strict requirements that make those adhering to them feel like they are accomplishing something before God. It makes them feel special and a little more holy than the rest. The requirements of Jesus might appear strict as well, but the difference is that they are always a fruit of intimacy with Him.

- *"You can't associate with that person"!* Religious voices will warn us against associating with unbelievers and to be careful with people who hold to a "wrong" theology on certain topics. The assumption is that when we spend time with these people, we will become defiled. When Jesus exhorts us to protect our boundaries by not giving everybody the same access to our life, it has nothing to do with the fear of becoming unclean. Boundaries is all about guarding our hearts.

- *"Don't eat that!"* Religion will create rules that relate to our lifestyle in certain areas that has nothing to do with our heart before God. For example, religion will make a big deal about food choices that please God. I'm all for a healthy diet and I encourage you to eat things that are good for your health. I have been practicing intermittent fasting for years now because it makes my health better. But it doesn't give me extra points with God.

- ***"You can't touch that!"*** Religion will put regulations in place concerning what you can touch. This isn't limited to physical touch, but it refers to what you touch with your life. These regulations will make the grey areas of life very black and white, suggesting that activities like sports or watching movies will make you less holy. This creates a defensive lifestyle based on fear. Of course, we should make wise choices concerning what we allow to influence our lives. There are certain things that are not good for our soul. However, there is a large grey area in these matters, so each one of us must be led by the Spirit.

### The Reward of Religion

Not only does religion possess these characteristics, but it comes with its own fleshly rewards. It makes its adherents feel special and a little more holy. Paul continues to write: *"These rules may seem wise because they require strong devotion, pious self-denial, and severe bodily discipline. But they provide no help in conquering a person's evil desires"* (Col. 2:23 NLT).

- ***"These rules may seem wise"***. Religion will make its practitioners appear wise and godly. The religious mind is always impressed by the zealot who creates a higher and stricter standard for "pleasing God". The reward for the religious person is that he or she usually appears to take life with God very seriously and in that way gains the admiration of people. The wisdom of Jesus always comes clothed in humility, which seldom appears very religious.

- *"They require strong devotion"*. Religion is not for the undisciplined people. It requires strength of will and an uncompromising devotion to fulfill religious programs. The people who have the strongest will and practices the most extreme asceticism become the heroes of religion. Sometimes Jesus will lead us into seasons where we live a more intense and disciplined life with the Father, but that is always an expression of or love for Him. In such seasons our willpower and performance will not be at the center, but the experience of the lavish love of the Father will.

- *"Pious self-denial"*. Religion has always celebrated the people who deny themselves the most. This is because in religion, having an intimate relationship with Jesus cannot be done while living an ordinary life. The people who really want to know God must deny their own human needs, such as marriage, hobbies, food and the good of life. As we live with Jesus, we will at times have to deny ourselves as well, but that is a fruit of us living in a fallen world where there are powers at work to resist the gospel. This is not a condition to gain His favor.

- *"Severe bodily discipline"*. Religion promises rewards for the people who can force their body to undergo hard discipline as a way of reaching God. The thought behind this is that our body, with its needs, is a hindrance to a relationship with God. Therefore, we need to be harsh with our bodies to be close to God. Jesus might lead us to fast and to adapt certain bodily disciplines at times as well, but that is an expression of our relationship with the Father, not a condition for it.

The things may not be wrong in themselves, but did you notice that something is missing here? Jesus is nowhere to be found! Religion makes us self-centered by focusing on doing things for Him. The gospel is about the life of Jesus flowing through us, not about us working for Him. Living in self-denial and choosing a more disciplined lifestyle is a good thing, if it is the fruit of our relationship with Jesus. Then it becomes a source of blessing, but if this becomes a self-centered project, it creates a lifestyle of dead works that traps us in legalism.

## The Catch of Religion

The problem is that even though a religious person lives a life of "wisdom" and self-denial, religion will leave us disappointed for this simple reason:

- *"But they provide no help in conquering a person's evil desires" (Col. 2:23).*

Only Jesus can transform and sanctify our lives. He doesn't want us to end up disillusioned by religious teachings. Let's ditch religion and instead trust wholeheartedly in our best Friend and Savior, Jesus Christ! In Him we will find freedom, both from religious guilt and a lifestyle in bondage to sin (Rom. 8:1-4).

# Activations

- Set aside 20-30 minutes for prayer. Ask the Holy Spirit to reveal more of how the jealousy of God is connected to His love. Ask Him to fill you with godly jealousy for Jesus. Write down what He speaks to you.

- Ask the Holy Spirit to reveal any mixture of law and grace within your life. Then repent from it and ask Him to deliver you from all religion and legalistic mindsets.

- If the Holy Spirit reveals areas of legalism and religion in your life, take a few moments to reflect on how this legalism came into your life. Invite the Holy Spirit to fill these areas with the grace and love of the Father.

- Read Col. 2:13-23 together with the Holy Spirit. Ask Him to reveal more of your freedom in Christ through these verses. Invite Him to show you the difference between legalistic disciplines and the spiritual disciplines that is a fruit of partnering with the love of Jesus Christ.

# CHAPTER 9: A HOLY AND SPOTLESS BRIDE

In the previous chapter we learned that we have died to the law, and that we are now married and united with Jesus. Because we are now united with Him, we have been made holy and complete through the cross. We are His perfect and spotless bride! Many believers have a hard time accepting this to be true and I was certainly one of them. I thought that I was messed up and that it was my fault that I had become that way. I was ashamed of being alive and I had perfected the art of condemnation by constantly focusing on my failures and sins. I did this because I carried a shame-based identity. Living in legalism always creates shame within the human heart. Unhealthy shame causes us to feel like there is something wrong with us. What a relief it was to discover that I had already been made holy and blameless in Christ and that I am now complete in Him!

## He Has Perfected Us

When our Father chose us, it was His plan to present us as a pure and innocent bride as a gift to His Son. The Father knew that we could never become holy enough by our own efforts, but He had already figured out how to make that happen. *"… he hath chosen us in him before the foundation of the world, that we should be holy and without blame before him in love" (Eph. 1:4).* Through the finished work of the cross, Jesus has perfected us for all time and made us blameless before the Father. Since we did not accomplish this through our good deeds, our bad behavior cannot undo it either. Our identity rests solely on the finished work of Christ. He gave us a new identity through His redemptive work on the cross. *"By the which will we are sanctified through the offering of the body of Jesus Christ once for all… For by one offering he hath perfected for ever them that are sanctified" (Hebr. 10:10, 14).* By doing this, Jesus has now made us into perfect sons and daughters before the Father. What the law could never do, Jesus accomplished by offering Himself. He made us perfect and holy before the Father forever!

## No More Self-Centeredness

One of the reasons why this is such good news, is that we have been delivered from the burden of analyzing our relationship with God. We never need to wonder if there are things blocking our relationship with the Father. For me, this revelation was a huge relief. I had adopted the habit of evaluating myself before God at the end of every day. I did this to make sure that I had no sins in my heart that was ruining my life with God. This might sound like a pretty godly habit, but the fruit of doing that was sin-consciousness and condemnation.

The fear of failure paralyzed me and I ended up as a very passive and fearful believer. I had managed to turn the good news of the gospel into the impossible task of making myself holy before God. Since I believed that there was something wrong with me, I always felt the need of trying to improve myself. But when I learned more about the finished work of Jesus Christ, I realized that what I tried to accomplish, He had already done. There is nothing wrong with us anymore because Jesus has purified and sanctified us through the cross.

## Living Out of Our Identity

When this revelation sunk into my heart, I entered a process where I slowly stopped living out of my old identity and instead learned to live as a new creation in Christ. I learned to embrace my new identity, which started a process of healing through which I could slowly accept that I'm a beloved and favored child of God. We have been raised to a new life in Christ, and we will find healing and freedom by knowing who we are in Him. This is the reason Paul made a point of trying to present every believer as complete in Christ. He knew that it is by embracing our identity in Christ that we'll find restoration and true freedom.

## This Transformed My Marriage

I have seen the powerful effects of embracing my identity in Christ in several areas of my life. Maybe the most important area was my marriage. Living under the law not only affect our own lives, but it affects how we treat the people we love as well. I was so bound by legalism that I has become like one of those religious watchmen from the Song of songs (see chapter 4). Because I had a lot of zeal for God but no revelation of the New Covenant, I thought that making Christian life work for me and my family was up to me. Living according to God's holy standard became my religious project, which included making sure that my wife lived up to "the biblical standard" of holiness. This was a tough season for my wife. She lived with the constant feeling of not being good enough for me. This created a lot of tension between us. I had placed our marriage under a religious yoke and my wife didn't like that. Fortunately, living under the law was such a burden that it wore me out. I ended up in a spiritual burnout where I didn't have the strength to strive anymore. That gave Jesus an opportunity to reach my heart.

Through the leading of the Holy Spirit, my wife and I gained a deeper insight into the New Covenant. We discovered that the holiness and perfection that we had been striving for was already ours in Christ. As we realized that we had been made complete in Jesus, we were slowly being delivered from religion and the pressure of living under the law. Discovering the New Covenant brought us on a journey of learning to live by the life of Christ. This revelation brought healing to our marriage by setting us free to live out of our identity in Christ. The beliefs of our hearts will eventually become our life and knowing that we have been made perfect in Christ, will cause purity and holiness to manifest in our lives.

### Presented as Complete in Christ

Paul wanted to present us as complete in Christ, by unveiling what Jesus had done to us through the finished work of the cross. *"Him we preach, warning every man and teaching every man in all wisdom, that we may present every man perfect in Christ Jesus. To this end I also labor, striving according to His working which works in me mightily" (Col. 1:28-29 NASB).* Knowing that we are perfect and holy before the Father heals the wound of shame and sets us free from carrying false guilt. This is important, because it is only then we can serve God in a way that brings life. We are called to be led by the Holy Spirit, not to be driven by guilt and a bad conscience. These are dead motives and dead motives produce dead works.

*For if the blood of goats and bulls, and the ashes of a heifer sprinkling those who have been defiled, sanctify for the cleansing of the flesh, how much more will the blood of Christ, who through the eternal Spirit offered Himself without blemish to God, cleanse your conscience from dead works to serve the living God (Hebr. 9:13-14 NASB)?*

The blood of Jesus cleanses our consciences from dead works so that we can serve the Father in freedom (You can find much more on this topic in my book *Abiding in the Father's Love*). The freedom of the Holy Spirit always manifests because of a revelation of our identity in Christ. Shame produces bondage and limitations in our life with God but knowing that we are complete through Jesus brings freedom to joyfully embrace our life with the Father.

As we are being delivered from shame and guilt, we are set free to live. It is important to understand that our Father loves life and that He wants us to live to the fullest. Jesus did not come to bring us an abundance of religious duties and obligations. He came to bring an abundance of life: *"The thief does not come except to steal, and to kill, and to destroy. I have come that they may have life, and that they may have it more abundantly"* (John 10:10 NKJV). There is so much hope and healing in knowing that there is nothing wrong with us anymore. God doesn't analyze our every move to point out our failures. As Jesus looks at His bride, He sees perfection and beauty because of the cross. If you have lived with shame and condemnation, you can invite the Holy Spirit to minister to your heart. The Father wants to heal every wound in our hearts, including the wounds caused by shame.

## Religion & the Mark of the Beast

The problem with religion is that it doesn't live *from* identity, but instead lives *for* identity. It tries to create a works-based identity before God through human strength. There is a famous passage in the book of Revelation that illustrates this truth. The passage I'm referring to is found in chapter 13, where a beast comes up out of the sea. This beast receives the full authority of Satan and it oppresses the nations. It even wage war against the saints. This beast, just like the great harlot is a picture of the religious spirit (Rev. 13:1-10).

Then a second beast comes up from the earth. This beast makes everyone take a mark on the right hand or forehead. It receives its power from the first beast, who arose from the sea. The second beast is a picture of the old man. The mark of the beast is the seal of the religious spirit (Rev. 13:12-15). The mark itself is the name of the beast or the number of his name:

*And he causes all, the small and the great, the rich and the poor, and the free and the slaves, to be given a mark on their right hands or on their foreheads, and he decrees that no one will be able to buy or to sell, except the one who has the mark, either the name of the beast or the number of his name. Here is wisdom. Let him who has understanding calculate the number of the beast, for the number is that of a man; and his number is six hundred and sixty-six" (Rev. 13:16-18 NASB).*

This mark is not a natural mark and neither is the number 666 a literal number. If it were, it would not have been written that the one with understanding will be able know its meaning. 666 is the number of man, representing human nature and the strength of the flesh. It is significant that this mark was taken either on the forehead or the right hand. The right hand is a picture of strength in the Scriptures (Exod. 15:6-7, Ps. 118:16). The forehead speaks of the mind of man, which is why God speaks of people that has a hard or impure forehead (Jer. 3:3, Ezek. 3:8). The mark of the beast was taken either on the right hand or the forehead. So, the mark of the beast is a picture of trusting the strength and wisdom of man.

This means that the people carrying the mark are those who put their trust in the strength and intelligence of man. They are living in the flesh, trusting in their own ability and mind when it comes to their life with Jesus. Only the people who received this mark could buy and sell. We noticed earlier how religion operates by negotiating with God through good works. When someone tries to become holy through their good works, that person is trusting in the strength of man to fulfill the will of God.

The people of Israel were commanded to wear the Word of God on their hand and to carry it on their forehead (Deut. 11:18). This was a sign that the people of God were to find their strength in the Word of God. Jesus is the living Word and He is our true source of strength. We don't need the mark of religion because we have been sealed by the Holy Spirit.

## Sealed by God

The book of Revelation speaks of another mark, that which the bondservants of Christ and the Father's children carry on their foreheads. This mark is called the seal of God and it is mentioned right after the mark of the beast as a contrast to it: *"Then I looked, and behold, the Lamb was standing on Mount Zion, and with Him 144,000 who had His name and the name of His Father written on their foreheads" (Rev. 14:1 NASB).* The 144 000 here is not meant to be taken literally, but it is a symbolic number. In this vision, John saw 12000 people from each of the twelve tribes. 12 is the number of completeness and 1000 is the number of all or fullness. Hence the 144 000 standing with the Lamb speaks of all God's people from all ages.

The Father gives this mark by writing His own name and the name of the Lamb on our forehead (Rev. 3:12, 7:3, 9:4). This is the same seal that Jesus received from the Father (John 6:27). We who have been marked with the seal of God are protected from the judgements that are being released in the book of Revelation. These judgements were executed against the realm of darkness and the religious spirit. But we are in Christ, and we have been delivered from the realm of darkness into the Kingdom of His beloved Son (Col. 1:13).

## Sealed by the Holy Spirit

In the letter to the Ephesians we find out what the seal of God is: *"In Him, you also, after listening to the message of truth, the gospel of your salvation—having also believed, you were sealed in Him with the Holy Spirit of the promise, who is a first installment of our inheritance, in regard to the redemption of God's own possession, to the praise of His glory"* (Eph. 1:13-14 NASB see also Eph. 4:30). We have been sealed with the Holy Spirit who has been given to us as a sign of redemption. As the bride of Christ, we are now living in the New Covenant, which is called *"the ministry of the Spirit"* (2 Cor. 3:8). This means that we are to live out of our new nature in Christ, trusting the Holy Spirit to empower us every day. We are the perfected and spotless bride of Christ and have the privilege of trusting Jesus Christ to live His life through us, empowering us to be and do everything that He has called us to be and do.

- Set aside 20-30 minutes for prayer. Ask the Holy Spirit to speak to bring more revelation on what it means that you have been made perfect and spotless in Christ. Write down the insights you receive from Him.

- Ask the Holy Spirit to reveal more on the difference between a shame-based identity and your identity as the bride of Christ. Then invite Jesus to minister healing to any area of shame in your life.

- How will your relationships change as you learn to live out of your identity in Christ? Ask the Holy Spirit to teach you how to live *from* your new identity on Christ instead of for it.

- We have been sealed by the Father. Ask the Holy Spirit to reveal more about what it means to be sealed by God and to take the mark of the beast. Write down any new insights you receive on this topic.

# CHAPTER 10: THE LORD IS A LOVING WARRIOR

The Lord is our Warrior and Champion. He will pick a fight with any principality or power who hold us captive, or who wants to seduce our hearts away from Him. Because Jesus loves us with a burning passion, He is very active in fighting our battles. Jesus is a warrior because He is a Lover. He wants to break all spiritual oppression and drive out all legalism from our lives. Miriam, the sister of Moses, sang a prophetic song of victory after the people of Israel had marched through the red sea. That song revealed that one of the Father's characteristics is that He is a warrior: *"The Lord is my strength and song, and He has become my salvation; This is my God, and I will praise Him; My father's God, and I will exalt Him. "The Lord is a warrior; The Lord is His name"* (Exod. 15:2-3 NASB).

The prophet Isaiah likewise declared that God is a warrior who is triumphing over all his enemies: *"The Lord will march out like a champion, like a warrior he will stir up his zeal; with a shout he will raise the battle cry and will triumph over his enemies"* (Isa. 42:13 NIV). That the Lord is a warrior explains how we have been made more than conquerors through Him who loves us. Jesus Himself is our champion who have triumphed over the enemy (Rom. 8:37).

In this chapter we will study how God has declared war against the realm of darkness by looking at the deliverance of Israel from the slavery of Egypt. This story reveals our Lord as a warrior and it gives a perfect illustration of how spiritual warfare is an act of divine love. Pharaoh is a type of Satan and Egypt represents the kingdom of darkness within this story. As we walk through the events leading up to Israel's deliverance, we'll find a picture of how our deliverance from the realm of darkness and spiritual oppression was accomplished through the cross: *"For He rescued us from the domain of darkness, and transferred us to the kingdom of*

*His beloved Son, in whom we have redemption, the forgiveness of sins"*
*(Col. 1:13-14 NASB).*

## The Cry of the Oppressed People of God

When the people of God suffer under demonic oppression and slavery, Jesus is not unmoved by the humiliation that spiritual captivity causes. He hears our cry for freedom and He has great compassion with the pain of His people (Exod. 2:23-25). When Israel was oppressed and enslaved in Egypt, God decided to do something about it, so He appeared to Moses in the burning bush and said:

*I have surely seen the oppression of My people who are in Egypt, and have heard their cry because of their taskmasters, for I know their sorrows. So I have come down to deliver them out of the hand of the Egyptians, and to bring them up from that land to a good and large land, to a land flowing with milk and honey (Exod. 3:7-8 NKJV).*

Not only did God want to deliver them from oppression, but He wanted to bring them into the promised land. Deliverance is never just about being set free from oppression, but the Father's goal is for us to step into greater freedom and blessing.

When studying the history of Israel, there are countless examples of how they ended up in bondage, which usually happened as a consequence of their disobedience and idolatry. As a result, they were being enslaved by the demonic powers behind these idols. When living under demonic oppression became too painful for them, they cried out to God who always responded by delivering and restoring them. This is something that we need to remember. It doesn't matter how deep we fall; God will always be faithful in forgiving and restoring us.

## Jesus Appears in Blazing Fire

We have already seen that Moses was a passionate lover of God, who immersed himself in the holy fire of God's love. Because Moses knew the love of God, he could become a deliverer of the people of Israel (Deut. 24:16-18). Already long before Moses encountered God at Sinai, he was familiar with the fire of God's love. The first time God was calling Moses to deliver His people, He appeared in a blazing fire. *"And the angel of the LORD appeared unto him in a flame of fire out of the midst of a bush: and he looked, and, behold, the bush burned with fire, and the bush was not consumed"* *(Exod. 3:2).* Usually when the Old Testament speaks about *"the angel of the Lord"* it refers to Jesus Himself, appearing in His pre-incarnate form. It makes sense for Jesus to appear at this moment, since He is always longing to deliver from oppression and evil (1 John 3:8). Jesus is our deliverance and breakthrough.

Here Jesus appeared in a blazing fire as a sign of His burning love for His people. Jesus later appeared to Moses multiple times. We know that Moses spoke to God face to face like a friend (Exod. 33:11). Yet, no one had seen the Father before Jesus came to reveal Him. But people had met Jesus in pre-incarnate form, which lead us to believe that Jesus appeared to speak to Moses in the tabernacle. In fact, we know that Moses found strength to endure as a leader because he carried a revelation of Christ.

## Moses Carried a Revelation of Jesus

Knowing that Moses carried a deep revelation of Jesus hundreds of years before the New Covenant was established, is fascinating. This revelation was more important to Moses than his reputation or his social status. His vision of Jesus gave him the strength to persevere through the many trials he faced, while he was leading the people of God into freedom.

*By faith Moses, when he had grown up, refused to be called the son of Pharaoh's daughter, choosing rather to endure ill-treatment with the people of God than to enjoy the temporary pleasures of sin, considering the reproach of Christ greater riches than the treasures of Egypt; for he was looking to the reward. (Hebr. 11:24-26 NASB).*

This reveals an important principle for anyone who has a calling to minister to the body of Christ. What qualifies us to be ministers of the New Covenant will always be a deep revelation of Jesus. Knowing Jesus is the only way to find strength to handle the pressure of leadership. We don't need to seek after leadership positions, we only need a deeper revelation of Christ. Knowing Jesus in a deeper way will make us leaders, because it will cause people to encounter Him through us. This is how we persevere in our calling: *"By faith he left Egypt, not fearing the wrath of the king; for he persevered, as though seeing Him who is unseen"* (Hebr. 11:27 NASB).

## Moses the Deliverer

As God was speaking to Moses, we can feel His love for His people. Jesus is always passionate for our freedom. This was His motivation when sending Moses to deliver the people of Israel: *"Now therefore, behold, the cry of the children of Israel has come to Me, and I have also seen the oppression with which the Egyptians oppress them. Come now, therefore, and I will send you to Pharaoh that you may bring My people, the children of Israel, out of Egypt"* (Exod. 3:9-10 NKJV). Moses was a bit reluctant to obey at first, feeling that he was unfit to be a leader because he was a bad speaker.
It seems like Moses was tormented by stage fright at this stage of his life (Exod. 4:10-17). In reality, *"Moses was learned in all the wisdom of the Egyptians, and was mighty in words and in deeds"* (Acts 7:22). But fear was still blinding Moses to his true identity at that moment in time.

I know how Moses felt when it comes to feeling inadequate as a speaker. Even though I'm now working as an itinerant minister, my worst fear used to be public speaking. Jesus set me free from this fear and I'm rarely nervous at all before speaking in public anymore. The good news is that there is freedom in knowing that the grace of God is enough for us (2 Cor. 12:9). When we give our weaknesses to God, the power of Jesus will rest upon us and His strength will manifest through our weakness.

God did not leave Moses alone in his struggles with fear. He sent Aaron to assist Moses by being his spokesman. God also gave Moses the ability to perform two signs from God to convince the people of Israel that God had sent him. He would be able to throw his staff on the ground and it would turn into a serpent, and he could make his hand white with leprosy by sticking it into his robe (Exod. 4:2-7). Signs and wonders serve an important function in our lives with God. They open the heart of people to receive the message that Jesus speaks through us and they reveal the heart of the Father. They are signs that create wonder within our hearts, revealing the beauty of Jesus. Aaron and Moses went before the people of Israel. As Moses performed the signs God had given to him, the people believed that he was sent by God (Exod. 4:29-31). Pharaoh was a little tougher to convince.

### The Hardening of Pharaoh's heart

God had already revealed to Moses that Pharaoh would remain unconvinced by these signs, since his magicians could duplicate them in a limited way. These signs were still showing God's superior power, since Moses' serpent ate the serpents brought forth the magicians. Pharaoh did not allow the children of Israel to leave, but instead chose to dramatically increase the pressure upon the people. God had *"... hardened the heart of Pharaoh, and he hearkened not unto them; as the LORD had spoken unto Moses"* (Exod.

*9:12).* The hardening of Pharaoh's heart is mentioned several times within this story. Sometimes, it says that God hardened Pharaoh's heart, while at other times the Scripture is telling us that Pharaoh hardened his own heart (Exod. 8:32, 10:20, 27, 11:10, 14:8). There is no contradiction in this. It simply means that God allowed Pharaoh to keep walking in his pride and idolatry.

The reason for this was that the deliverance of the people of Israel included God's war and judgement against the Egyptian gods. As we saw earlier, Jesus is jealous for His people. He will wage war against any spiritual power that tries to steal the heart of His beloved. But He will pick a fight with the false gods whenever they oppress or enslaves His bride as well. When God initiates deliverance from oppression, the response of the demonic realm is usually like that of Pharaoh. The devil increases the pressure and make the burdens of slavery even heavier, hoping that we're going to grow tired and give up. We shouldn't fall for that simple strategy. An increase of demonic resistance means that the devil is nervous. He knows that he will lose the battle and he increase the pressure in a desperate attempt to make us quit. We can be certain that as we are standing firm in Christ, deliverance will come, because no evil can resist the power of Jesus Christ.

**The Plagues of Egypt and the Judgement Against the Gods**

God had decided that he deliverance of God's people was to be accomplished through ten plagues. Each one of these ten plagues was a judgement against one of the gods of Egypt to demonstrate God's superior power. In the following scripture, we can see how God told Moses that *"…against all the gods of Egypt I will execute judgments—I am the Lord. The blood shall be a sign for you on the houses where you live; and when I see the blood I will pass over you, and no plague will come upon you to destroy you when I strike the land of Egypt"* Exod. 12:12-13 NASB). While God executed judgement against the gods of Egypt, the children of Israel were going to be protected and delivered by the blood of the Passover lamb. This is a powerful picture of how the blood of Jesus has delivered us from both death and the power of the devil.

## The Ten Plagues

We are now going to take a brief look at each of these plagues to study how God delivered Israel by judging the gods of Egypt. These judgements were executed to demonstrate the superior power of God over the demonic powers. This is a foreshadowing of the ultimate victory of Jesus on the cross, where He disarmed and stripped the principalities and powers of all authority:

1.  ***The water of the Nile River turned into blood (Exod. 7:14-25).*** The first plague that God released upon Egypt was that of turning the water to blood. When Aaron touched the river with his rod, it immediately turned to blood and all the fish died. This caused a terrible stench as the river smelled of death. Partially able to duplicate this miracle, the magicians of Pharaoh also turned water into blood, leaving him unconvinced by this sign from God. For seven days the water throughout all the land of Egypt remained like this, being totally unsuitable for drinking. This was the perfect length of time to demonstrate that the Lord was superior to all the other gods of Egypt. This was the judgement of God upon *Hapi, the God of the Nile River.*

2.  ***The plague of frogs (Exod. 8:1-15).*** The second plague that came upon Egypt, was that of frogs. Frogs came up from the river and spread until they appeared everywhere. They could be found in homes, clothes

and even in the food of the Egyptians. From the least to the greatest, no one in Egypt could escape being hit by this plague. Pharaoh's magicians were able to make similar frogs appear as they tried to imitate the power of the Lord, but only Moses could make the frogs disappear from the land. Through this plague, the Lord executed judgement against *the Egyptian goddess of fertility and childbirth, Heqet.*

3.  **The Plague of the gnats (Exod. 8:16-19).** Aaron was smiting the dust with his rod and the dust became gnats spreading throughout all the land. These gnats descended on both people and animal. Pharaoh's magicians now had to admit defeat, being unable to compete with the manifested power of God, which was much greater than the powers that they received from their Egyptian gods. They had to profess: *"This is the finger of God" (Exod. 8:19).* This third plague was God's judgement against the Egyptian god *Geb, the god of the earth.*

4.  **The Plague of the Swarms of Flies (Exod. 8:20-32).** This plague caused swarms of flies to overwhelm Egypt, leaving it totally wasted. This plague only affected the Egyptians, while the children of Israel remained unscathed. Plagued by the flies, Pharaoh now tried to bargain with the Lord, by pretending to allow the people to go to worship God, but only if they worshiped and sacrificed within the land of Egypt. Pharaoh pretended to give up solely to have Moses ask the Lord that the swarms of flies may depart. But as soon as this request was answered by God and the flies departed, Pharaoh hardened his heart and turned back on his promise again. He still

wasn't ready to concede and let them go. Pharaoh continued to worship the gods of Egypt even though the power of the God of Israel was clearly superior to the Egyptian gods. Through this plague God executed judgement upon *Khepri, the god of creation and rebirth.*

5. ***The Plague where the Egyptian livestock died (Exod. 9:1-7).*** This plague caused disease and pestilence to fall upon the livestock in Egypt. It was so severe that it caused them to die. This affected the Egyptians by creating a disaster in areas such as food, farming and economic goods that were produced through these livestock. Still Pharaoh's heart remained hard and he would not humble himself and listen to the Lord, but instead kept on worshipping the Egyptian gods and goddesses. Pharaoh became a real-life example that pride goes before destruction (Prov. 16:18). This was the judgement of God against *Hathor, the Egyptian goddess of love, motherhood and protection.*

6. ***The Plague of Boils (Exod. 9:8-12).*** The sixth plague struck Egypt in the form of a terrible sickness. Being instructed by the Lord, Moses took ashes from the brick kiln and threw them into the air. As the dust spread all over Egypt, it settled on man and beast alike, in the form of boils and sores. Cleanliness was important in the Egyptian society, so this plague in essence caused the whole people to become unclean. Even the magicians were unable to perform their usual rituals to their Egyptian gods. They couldn't even appear before Pharaoh. Moses and Aaron were the only ones left standing in front of Pharaoh, as they were being strengthened and supported by the

Lord Himself. This plague was the judgement of God upon *Isis, the Egyptian goddess of healing, medicine and magic.*

7. ***The Plague of Hails and fire (Exod. 9:13-35).*** Hail of unspeakable ability to destroy, rained down from the sky and turned to fire when hitting the ground. The crops that were destroyed by the hail consisted of flax and barley, which were ripening in the fields. This destruction made life more miserable, but as far as effecting the food supply, the wheat still survived. This gave the Egyptians still another chance to turn to God and forsake their own Egyptian gods and goddesses. God is merciful and He will always give a second and third chance. Through this plague, God was executing judgement against *Nut, the Egyptian goddess of the sky and the heavens.*

8. ***The Plague of Locust Swarms (Exod. 10:1-20).*** This is the second wave of destruction to follow the hail, and whatever crops were left untouched by the hail and fire, they were completely consumed by the swarms of locusts that descended from the sky.
This plague affected the Egyptians' life source in a disastrous way. By hitting their food supply, God displayed the possibility of eminent death if Pharaoh remained hardened in heart. But Pharaoh still didn't concede. Through this plague, God pronounced judgement upon *Seth, the Egyptian god of war, storms and chaos.*

9. *Darkness covered the land (Exod. 10:21-29).* This plague caused darkness to fall upon the land. Egypt descended into three days of deep darkness, which covered the whole nation. The sun gave no light and the Lord showed His power over the sun. This was a clear sign that the God of Israel had ultimate power over life and death. The impact of this plague shook both the psychological and religious worldview of the Egyptians. To the Egyptians, darkness spoke of death, judgment and hopelessness. Darkness was a complete absence of light. Through this plague, God executed judgement against *Ra, the Egyptian sun god.*

10. *Death of the firstborn sons of Egypt (Exod. 12:29-32).* The angel of death walked through the land of Egypt claiming the life of every firstborn Egyptian son, all throughout the land. All Egyptian households were grieving that night, even Pharaoh himself. This time, the Egyptians drove out the people of Israel and they were finally delivered from the oppression of Egypt. This was the last plague and it was God's judgement upon the most worshipped God in Egypt, *Pharaoh, who was believed to be the ultimate power of Egypt.*

### Delivered by the Blood of the Lamb

We have already seen how the people of Israel were protected and delivered from death and oppression by the blood of the Passover lamb. As God was about to release the final plague, He commanded Israel to celebrate the first Passover by sacrificing a spotless lamb. They were commanded to eat the Lamb the same night and then take of its blood to smear on their doorframes.

*Announce to the whole community of Israel that on the tenth day of this month each family must choose a lamb or a young goat for a sacrifice, one animal for each household... The animal you select must be a one-year-old male, either a sheep or a goat, with no defects... They are to take some of the blood and smear it on the sides and top of the doorframes of the houses where they eat the animal (Exod 12:3, 5, 7 NLT).*

The Passover lamb was, of course, a type of Jesus Christ, the Lamb of God. *"For Christ our Passover Lamb has been sacrificed" (1 Cor. 5:7 AMP).* Through His blood, we have been delivered from all judgement, as well as from sin and the power of evil. Jesus Christ is our warrior and champion, who has won the spiritual battle for us. We overcome by standing in His victory. This is the reason that God told Moses: *"But the blood on your doorposts will serve as a sign, marking the houses where you are staying. When I see the blood, I will pass over you. This plague of death will not touch you when I strike the land of Egypt" (Exod. 12:13 NLT).*

Jesus is the victorious warrior, and He is our Passover Lamb, who delivers us through His blood (Rev. 12:11). Jesus won a complete and permanent victory by laying down His life for us. Because Jesus loves us, He will never leave us in oppression. He will fight to bring us into the land of promise, where we can live in the fullness of all the blessings that He won for us through His redemptive work on the cross.

**Activations**

- Set aside 20-30 minutes for prayer. Ask the Holy Spirit to unveil more of the nature of Jesus as the Lord our warrior. Write down what He reveals to you.

- Moses endured in His calling to be a deliverer of God's people because of his revelation of Jesus. Ask the Holy Spirit to unveil more of the heart of Jesus to you, so that you can endure in your calling as well.

- Jesus is our Passover Lamb that delivered us from the power of the devil by his blood. Invite the Holy Spirit to reveal more of this aspect of the cross, and to set you free from any spiritual oppression or bondage.

- Take some time in prayer and ask the Father to anoint you with the power of the Holy Spirit to bring freedom and deliverance to God's people. Jesus wants to reveal Himself as a loving warrior through you. Ask Him for the grace to partner with Him in that.

# CHAPTER 11: THE OVERCOMING BRIDE

From the previous chapter we know that Jesus is a warrior who fights our battles. The truth is that Jesus has already defeated all the powers of darkness. He is our victorious champion, and as His bride, we stand in His victory. We overcome because we are born of God. Being overcomers is part of our New Creation DNA. We will face battles and challenges in life and even though God has prepared a victorious future for us together with Jesus, life is tough at times. We live in a fallen world that lies under the power of the devil. This means that we will face spiritual attacks and the consequences of the law of sin and death operating in this world (Rom. 5:12). The good news is that we have been made partakers of divine nature, which makes it part of our new nature to overcome. Jesus leads us forth in triumph and victory. *"But thanks be to God, who always leads us in triumph in Christ, and through us spreads and makes evident everywhere the sweet fragrance of the knowledge of Him" (2 Cor. 2:14 AMP).*

## We Overwhelmingly Conquer

Sometimes people think that teaching on new creation realities denies the problems of life, or that living as the victorious bride implies that we will walk through life without pain. That is either a big misunderstanding or a deliberate misrepresentation. It is a caricature of the biblical teaching on faith. All of us will face the storms of life and spiritual attacks, but Jesus has promised that we will overcome these storms in victory by abiding in His love.

*Who will separate us from the love of Christ? Will tribulation, or trouble, or persecution, or famine, or nakedness, or danger, or sword? Just as it is written: "For Your sake we are killed all day long; We were regarded as sheep to be slaughtered." But in all these things we overwhelmingly conquer through Him who loved us (Rom. 8:35-37 NASB).*

Paul writes that in all these things we *"overwhelmingly conquer"* through Him who loved us. There are two important lessons to learn from this scripture. The first one is that when Paul writes *"in all these things"*, he means the tribulations of life. Tribulations will come in all shapes and sizes, but none of them has the power to separate us from the love of God. The second lesson that we learn is that we conquer *"through Him who loved us"*. As we are being rooted and grounded in the love of Christ, we find grace and strength to overcome in all things. *"Yet even in the midst of all these things, we triumph over them all, for God has made us to be more than conquerors, and his demonstrated love is our glorious victory over everything" (Rom. 8:37 TPT)!* The clearest way in which the Father has revealed His love for us, is by Jesus dying on the cross. But Jesus will demonstrate His love for us in a personal way as well. As we learn to abide in Christ, we become rooted and grounded in His love, which gives us strength to overcome. The revelation of His love is our victory.

### Why Do We Need to Overcome?

Many times, people ask how it is possible that the world looks like it does if God is good. Why do we have to live in a world where it is necessary for us to overcome? The challenges that we are facing do not enter our lives because God is powerless to do something about them. Neither is it His will for our lives to be ruined by evil. But because God has given an amount of free will, both to man and other spiritual beings, the choices that we make affect this world in a very real way. We can choose to partner with the will of God, or we can choose to cooperate with evil in this world. It was through Adam's choice that evil entered the world in the first place: *"Therefore, just as through one man sin entered into the world, and death through sin, and so death spread to all mankind, because all sinned"* (Rom. 5:12 NASB). Because of the choice Adam made, the world is right now under the influence of the destructive forces of sin and death. This is why the world is in such a messed-up state. When man fell into sin, death entered this world. Adam had been given authority to steward the earth, but he handed that authority over to Satan. Until Jesus comes back, Satan now has legal right to operate in this world. *"We know that we are of God, and that the whole world lies in the power of the evil one"* (1 John 5:19 NASB). The world is now under the influence of the devil. Satan is called the god of this world, and he reigns through the law of sin and death (2 Cor. 4:3-4). This is the reason why evil things can happen in the world even though God is good and this is why we are called to be overcomers.

## We Have Been Set Free from Sin and Death

Even though sin and death have been released into this world through the fall, we have been delivered from being under their influence. *"Therefore, there is now no condemnation for those who are in Christ Jesus, because through Christ Jesus the law of the Spirit who gives life has set you free from the law of sin and death"* (Rom. 8:1-2 NIV). Through Jesus Christ we are now under the influence of another law, the law of the Spirit who gives life. Instead of being ruled by the power of sin, we are now filled with the life of the Holy Spirit. We are living in Christ, where there is no death or darkness. This means that we are now living in a realm where darkness has no influence.

## Delivered into the Kingdom of Christ

We live in the sphere where darkness has no power over us. Jesus rescued us from death, which is the sphere within the spiritual realm where darkness has the right to operate. *"For he has rescued us from the dominion of darkness and brought us into the kingdom of the Son he loves" (Col. 1:13 NIV).* We are living in the kingdom of God under the lordship of Jesus Christ. The kingdom of God is the realm where God rules. This realm is the place where life and righteousness have been established. This means that we live in a dimension where darkness is powerless. We have been seated with Jesus in heavenly places to reign in life with Him.

## We Are the Ones Who Overcome

In the book of Revelation, we find seven letters, written to seven churches in Asia minor. The book of Revelation was written to reveal the victory of Christ, and these letters were placed within this book to encourage the bride of Christ in all places and times throughout the history of the church. Within these letters, Jesus promises *"the one who overcomes"* seven different rewards. These overcomers are not a special class of believers, but they simply refer to us who are His bride. We have already seen how we overwhelmingly conquer through the love of Christ. The book of Revelation expresses the same truth with these words:

*Now salvation, and strength, and the kingdom of our God, and the power of His Christ have come, for the accuser of our brethren, who accused them before our God day and night, has been cast down. And they overcame him by the blood of the Lamb and by the word of their testimony, and they did not love their lives to the death (Rev. 12:10-11 NKJV).*

We overcome because we are in Christ. The blood of Jesus has delivered us from our sins and He has defeated the devil through the cross. Because we are in Christ, we now stand in His victory. Notice that every passage addressing *"the one who overcomes"*, encourages us to hear what the Spirit speaks to the churches. The message of the Holy Spirit to the bride is not hard to understand.

The Holy Spirit always glorifies Jesus and His finished work on the cross. *"He shall glorify me: for he shall receive of mine, and shall shew it unto you" (John 16:14).* The Holy Spirit glorifies Jesus by revealing our victory in Christ! We are now going to look briefly at each of the seven passages addressing *"the one who overcomes"*.

## The Overcoming Bride in Ephesus

*"The one who has an ear, let him hear what the Spirit says to the churches. To the one who overcomes, I will grant to eat from the tree of life, which is in the Paradise of God" (Rev. 2:7 NASB).*

The tree of Life grows in the Paradise of God and we know that the tree of Life is a picture of Jesus Christ. He speaks of Himself as the Life (John 14:6). Only through Jesus does man receive eternal life. But that life not only means that we will live forever. It means that we now are free to enjoy God's own quality of life in abundance (John 10:10). Jesus Christ indwells us, which means that the tree of Life is planted in the secret place of our heart. Through fellowshipping with Jesus, we can eat from fruit of the tree of life whenever we want.

## The Overcoming Bride in Smyrna

*"The one who has an ear, let him hear what the Spirit says to the churches. The one who overcomes will not be hurt by the second death" (Rev. 2:11 NASB).*

The second death means to be thrown in the lake of fire, where all evil, including sin, death and the devil will meet its end. This same fate awaits those who have not received Jesus as Lord and Savior. They don't have eternal life and at judgement day they will be thrown into the lake of fire and perish (Rev. 20:11-14, 21:8). We are overcomers because we have received eternal life in Christ and the second death has no power over us. *"Blessed and holy is the one who has a part in the first resurrection; over these the second death has no power, but they will be priests of God and of Christ, and will reign with Him for a thousand years"* (Rev. 20:6 NASB). The thousand years of reigning with Christ is not a literal thousand years, but this is a symbolic number meaning forever. In the Scriptures, the number thousand usually means all, endless or ever increasing. For example, the Psalms speaks of God owning the cattle on the thousand hills (Ps. 50:10). This doesn't mean that God owns the cattle only on a thousand hills, but that He owns them all. In the same way, when it is written that we will reign with Jesus for a thousand years, it means that the bride will reign with Him forever.

### The Overcoming Bride in Pergamum

*"The one who has an ear, let him hear what the Spirit says to the churches. To the one who overcomes, I will give some of the hidden manna, and I will give him a white stone, and a new name written on the stone which no one knows except the one who receives it"* (Rev. 2:17 NASB).

Jesus speaks of Himself as the Bread of Life (John 6:32-35). By eating of Him, we share in His life. We eat the hidden manna whenever we fellowship with Jesus. We have been given a white stone with a new name as well. This name refers to our personal identity in Christ. Our family name is "in Christ". We belong to the Father's family and we have a corporate identity, but we also have a first name. That name describes our calling, gifting, and personality. In short, it reveals everything that is unique about how God created us. Abraham is an example of this. His name was Abram, but when God revealed that Abram was going to be a father of many nations, He changed his name to Abraham (Gen. 17:1-16). We can access our personal identity in Christ by eating the Bread of Life. In the presence of Jesus, the Father's purpose for our lives becomes clear!

## The Overcoming Bride in Thyatira

*"The one who overcomes, and the one who keeps My deeds until the end, I will give him authority over the nations; and he shall rule them with a rod of iron, as the vessels of the potter are shattered, as I also have received authority from My Father; and I will give him the morning star. The one who has an ear, let him hear what the Spirit says to the churches" (Rev. 2:26-29 NASB).*

The bride of Christ has received authority to rule and reign over the nations. We have a greater destiny than just making disciples *in* all nations. Jesus has told us to make disciples *of* all nations (Matt. 28:18-20). Jesus is the desire of all nations because only He can shepherd the nations, providing the prosperity and peace that every nation needs (Hagg. 2:7). Only Jesus can heal and fully restore the soul of a nation. *"On each side of the river grew a tree of life, bearing twelve crops of fruit, with a fresh crop each month. The leaves were used for medicine to heal the nations" (Rev. 22:2 NLT).* We have not received authority to rule by the strength of man, but to represent the heart of Jesus through self-giving love, godly wisdom and the power of the Holy Spirit. We are called to bring healing to the nations together with Jesus.

## The Overcoming Bride in Sardis

*"The one who overcomes will be clothed the same way, in white garments; and I will not erase his name from the book of life, and I will confess his name before My Father and before His angels. The one who has an ear, let him hear what the Spirit says to the churches" (Rev. 3:5-6 NASB).*

As the bride of Christ, we are now clothed in white garments, referring to us being the righteousness of God in Christ (2 Cor. 5:21). This means that our innocence has been restored and that we are not stained by sin anymore. We did nothing to earn our new identity, but we simply received it by grace through faith in Jesus Christ (Eph. 2:8). Our names will remain in the book of Life forever. Jesus is not ashamed to call us brothers. He will gladly confess our names before His Father (Hebr. 2:11). After all, we are His pure and beloved bride.

### The Overcoming Bride in Philadelphia

*"The one who overcomes, I will make him a pillar in the temple of My God, and he will not go out from it anymore; and I will write on him the name of My God, and the name of the city of My God, the new Jerusalem, which comes down out of heaven from My God, and My new name. The one who has an ear, let him hear what the Spirit says to the churches" (Rev. 3:12-13 NASB).*

The people walking in their bridal identity will become pillars in the temple of God. That means that they will become strong leaders who carry the work of God in the power of the Holy Spirit. True leaders are always formed within the chambers of intimate union with Christ (2 Cor. 1:9). From that place, they gain God's perspective and they will be able to lead the people of God further into the Father's heart. The name of Jesus will be written upon us, as well as the name of the city of God. We have already seen that we are the New Jerusalem, since this is the wife of the Lamb (Rev. 21:2, 9-11). We will be marked by the name of Jesus because we are His. We will be marked by the name of the city of God as well because that is who we are.

## The Overcoming Bride in Laodicea

*"The one who overcomes, I will grant to him to sit with Me on My throne, as I also overcame and sat with My Father on His throne. The one who has an ear, let him hear what the Spirit says to the churches"* (Rev. 3:21-22).

We are seated with Christ in the heavenly places, at the right hand of the Father, and we are now reigning in life with Jesus (Eph. 2:6, Rom. 5:17). We are overcomers because we stand in His victory. We have authority to rule and reign with Him. All our enemies are under our feet because we are in Christ. *"Behold, I give unto you power to tread on serpents and scorpions, and over all the power of the enemy: and nothing shall by any means hurt you. Notwithstanding in this rejoice not, that the spirits are subject unto you; but rather rejoice, because your names are written in heaven"* (Luke 10:19-20).

## We Are Those Who Overcome

It is not complicated to understand who the overcomers are. We who are in Christ are *"those who overcome"*. To be the overcoming bride is our identity and the promises given to us speak of our inheritance in Him (Rom 8:17). All of this belongs to us now. We have the tree of life within us, and the second death has no power over us. We are the overcomers who reign in life, together with Jesus. *"For if by the one man's offense death reigned through the one, much more those who receive abundance of grace and of the gift of righteousness will reign in life through the One, Jesus Christ"* (Rom. 5:17 NKJV).

- Set aside 20-30 minutes for prayer. Ask the Holy Spirit to reveal more of your nature as an overcomer, as well as how you overcome through the love of Jesus Christ. Write down the insights that He gives to you.

- All of us are going through trials and spiritual battles at times. How does your perspective on spiritual battles change when you know that you're an overcomer?
Ask the Holy Spirit to give more insight concerning the overcoming life.

- Go back and read the part of this chapter that lists the blessings to the overcomers in the seven churches. Ask the Holy Spirit to highlight one of these churches as you read. Then read the whole letter to that specific church and invite the Holy Spirit to speak to you. You'll find the letters to the seven churches in the book of Revelation chapter two and three. Write down what He reveals.

- Take time in prayer to ask the Father for an anointing to encourage and inspire the body of Christ to overcome. You are called to support your fellow believers who are right now going through a spiritual battle. Ask the Holy Spirit to empower you in doing that.

# CHAPTER 12: JESUS IS THE FAITHFUL BRIDEGROOM

One of the most beautiful characteristics of Jesus Christ is His faithfulness. His commitment is never dependent on our amount of obedience to Him, but always on His faithful love for us. *"If we are faithless, He remains faithful; He cannot deny Himself"* (2 Tim. 2:13 NKJV). The faithfulness of God is one of the major themes of the Bible. When reading the Old Testament, we find that God was patient and faithful to His people, even while they chose to abandon Him and fell into apostasy. The New Testament, as well as church history, tells a similar story. It shows us how Jesus has remained faithful to His bride through both good and bad times. Jesus is rightly called *"… the faithful witness, and the first begotten of the dead, and the prince of the kings of the earth"* (Rev. 1:5). He will never give up on us and he will finish the good work that He has begun within our lives (Phil. 1:6).

I could give countless testimonies from my own life about the faithfulness of Jesus. My journey with God is a huge testimony of His mercy and faithfulness to me in the midst of my weakness and failures. It is more than obvious to me that the Father didn't chose me because I was qualified enough to fulfill my calling in His kingdom. He chose me to demonstrate His faithfulness by making me a trophy of grace. This insight makes me enormously grateful. Knowing His faithfulness and my weaknesses serves as a daily reminder for me to stay humble and take the low road.

## Chosen Out of Sheer Love

In many ways, the history of the body of Christ is a replay of the history of Israel. In fact, it was to demonstrate His grace and love that God chose Israel as His people: *"The Lord did not set his heart on you and choose you because you were more numerous than other nations, for you were the smallest of all nations! Rather, it was simply that the Lord loves you, and he was keeping the oath he had sworn to your ancestors"* (Deut. 7:7-8 NLT). This was how it all began for Israel. God embraced them out of sheer love. He loves to call the people who are overlooked and oppressed to Himself, raising them up and revealing them as trophies of His grace. Our story, both personal and corporate, has always been a testimony of the Father choosing us out of sheer love. He is merciful to us, even though we have done nothing to deserve it. By doing so, He has given eternal proof of His goodness and faithfulness.

### No Reason for Boasting

The Father has chosen us out of His sheer love and grace. He didn't choose us because of our special qualities. The only reason that we can become the people we are called to be, is because of the faithfulness of Jesus. *"Take a good look, friends, at who you were when you got called into this life. I don't see many of "the brightest and the best" among you, not many influential, not many from high-society families"* (1 Cor. 1:26 The Message). I have already addressed this passage thoroughly in my previous books, but we need to look at this scripture to see the faithfulness of the Father towards us. He deliberately chooses people that were doomed to fail in the natural. The Father basically chose the least qualified people He could find for an impossible task. Here is the reason for Him doing so:

*Isn't it obvious that God deliberately chose men and women that the culture overlooks and exploits and abuses, chose these "nobodies" to expose the hollow pretensions of the "somebodies"? That makes it quite clear that none of you can get by with blowing your own horn before God (1 Cor. 1:27-29 The Message).*

We have nothing to boast about whatsoever, other than being chosen out of sheer love by our heavenly Father. He wants to use nobodies like us to expose the empty pretentions of this world. The only thing we can boast in, is the grace and mercy of Jesus Christ amid our failures and shortcomings. He is a faithful Savior and friend. *"Everything that we have—right thinking and right living, a clean slate and a fresh start—comes from God by way of Jesus Christ. That's why we have the saying, "If you're going to blow a horn, blow a trumpet for God" (1 Cor. 1:28-31 The Message).*

## The Prophet Hosea Marries a Prostitute

There is one person who was called to reflect the faithfulness of Jesus to an unfaithful bride in a radical way. That man was the prophet Hosea. We can read his story in the book that bears his name. The name Hosea means *salvation* or *deliverer*. This is a fitting name since Hosea was called to be a prophetic picture of Jesus as our faithful bridegroom. His life became a sign that was pointing to God's everlasting love and faithfulness towards His unfaithful people:

*When the Lord first began speaking to Israel through Hosea, he said to him, "Go and marry a prostitute, so that some of her children will be conceived in prostitution. This will illustrate how Israel has acted like a prostitute by turning against the Lord and worshiping other gods."*
*So Hosea married Gomer, the daughter of Diblaim, and she became pregnant and gave Hosea a son (Hos. 1:2-3 NLT).*

This marriage between Hosea and Gomer, the prostitute, was to be a prophetic parable, illustrating the idolatry of the people of Israel. Hosea was a picture of God, while Gomer was a picture of the Israelites.

## Their Children Were Given Prophetic Names

Hosea and Gomer had three children together. God told Hosea that each one of them was to be given a name with prophetic significance. Each of these names were signs pointing to God's temporal rejection and judgement of Israel. They were to be sent into exile because of their idolatry (Hos. 1:4-9). It even looked like Israel had burnt their last chance, but God was not yet finished with Israel.

## Temporal Rejection Turned into Restoration

Because of their idolatry, Israel reaped a temporal rejection. But because of the faithfulness of Jesus, the house of Israel will reap salvation and restoration. *"Yet the number of the children of Israel shall be as the sand of the sea, which cannot be measured or numbered. And it shall come to pass in the place where it was said to them, 'You are not My people,' There it shall be said to them, 'You are sons of the living God (Hos. 1:10 NKJV).* Even though Israel had given themselves to idolatry and had broken their covenant with their God, He remained faithful to them, and Hosea prophesied about their coming restoration where they will finally welcome their Messiah: *"Then the children of Judah and the children of Israel shall be gathered together, and appoint for themselves one head; And they shall come up out of the land, for great will be the day of Jezreel"* (Hos. 1:11 *NKJV)!* This is being fulfilled whenever one of them receive Jesus as their Messiah and become a part of the Israel of God. There is a massive harvest of souls coming from the children of Judah, as Jesus is being unveiled to them as their true Messiah. God always stays faithful to His promises.

It is important for us to remember that God is faithful to His promises towards us as well. We all make stupid choices at times and sometimes these choices will take us to places where we feel exiled from the calling of God upon our lives. I have spoken to many believers who feel as though they have lost their calling because of sin and personal failure. I have good news for those of you who feel that way. God will never take back His gifts and callings from you, not even when you fail: *"For the gifts and calling of God are without repentance" (Rom 11:29).* Our calling has never rested on the shaky foundation of our faithfulness to God. His purposes with us rest on the sure foundation of the faithfulness of Jesus Christ! The gifts and callings of God are irrevocable. We can trust in Him to make His plans for you come to pass in His time.

## We Have Been Redeemed

Gomer was unfaithful to Hosea, just like Israel were unfaithful to God. *"Then the Lord said to me, "Go and love your wife again, even though she commits adultery with another lover. This will illustrate that the Lord still loves Israel, even though the people have turned to other gods and love to worship them" (Hos. 3:1 NLT).* Even though Gomer was unfaithful to Hosea, he still loved her and remained faithful to her. In the same way, our Bridegroom Jesus Christ, remains faithful to us, even though we have been unfaithful to Him. Hosea acted out this prophetic parable by buying her back:

*"So I bought her back for fifteen pieces of silver and five bushels of barley and a measure of wine. Then I said to her, "You must live in my house for many days and stop your prostitution. During this time, you will not have sexual relations with anyone, not even with me" (Hos. 3:2-4 NLT).*

Hosea became Gomer's redeemer by paying for her freedom. He brought her back into his house and her lovers could no longer reach her. Gomer was delivered and cleansed from her old ways. This is a picture of how Jesus is faithful to redeem, forgive, and restore His unfaithful bride. Just like Hosea became the deliverer of Gomer by paying for her freedom, so Jesus has saved us by buying our freedom through the cross: *"But he that is joined unto the Lord is one spirit… What? know ye not that your body is the temple of the Holy Ghost which is in you, which ye have of God, and ye are not your own? For ye are bought with a price: therefore glorify God in your body, and in your spirit, which are God's"* (1 Cor. 6:17, 19-20).

## Delivered & Restored by Jesus Christ

As we keep on reading the prophetic story of Hosea and Gomer, we notice that after he had bought her back, she was commanded to abstain from sexual relationships for a period of time, even with Hosea her husband. This was an illustration of how Israel was to live through a season of barrenness.

*This shows that Israel will go a long time without a king or prince, and without sacrifices, sacred pillars, priests, or even idols! But afterward the people will return and devote themselves to the Lord their God and to David's descendant, their king. In the last days, they will tremble in awe of the Lord and of his goodness"* (Hos. 3:2-5 NLT).

Notice the promise of God. This sad but captivating story does not end on a sad note. It ends with restoration and joy as God reveals how Israel will return to Him, with a promise that when they do, Israel will be embraced by their Messiah, Jesus Christ.

Our story will have a happy ending as well. Even though we might have been stuck in a cycle of rebellion and failure, Jesus remains faithful. He keeps on pursuing us until He finally gets what He wants. Jesus will have a pure and faithful bride who will live with Him in a union of love for all eternity! *"'Come. I will show you the beautiful bride, the wife of the Lamb.' He carried me away in the realm of the Spirit to the top of a great, high mountain. There he showed me the holy city, Jerusalem, descending out of heaven from God" (Rev. 21:9-10 TPT).*

## Our Union with Jesus Foreshadowed in Hosea

God gave Hosea the grace to look into His future and the prophet saw the season in which we live. God gave him prophetic visions of the New Covenant and our union with Jesus. When reading these visions, we find some amazing promises, pointing to the union between Jesus and His bride. These promises are our inheritance and we can enjoy their fulfillment today. Remember that we are in union with Jesus right now and that we can walk in the full blessing of being one with Him at this moment. Therefore, the following verses describe our present relationship with Jesus:

*"Therefore, behold, I am going to persuade her, bring her into the wilderness, and speak kindly to her. "Then I will give her her vineyards from there, And the Valley of Achor as a door of hope. And she will respond there as in the days of her youth, as in the day when she went up from the land of Egypt. "And it will come about on that day," declares the Lord, "That you will call Me my husband and no longer call Me my Baal (Hos. 2:14-16 NASB).*

Jesus sometimes brings us out into hidden places to speak words of kindness to us. The New Covenant reveals the gentleness and lovingkindness of Jesus. The words He speaks bring healing and restoration to our soul. Jesus will sometimes lead us out into the wilderness of intimacy and grace. He does that to silence all the other voices and opinions competing for our attention. He leads us back into the vineyard of intimacy, where we are renewed and restored by His presence.

## Jesus is Our Door of Hope

We read that Jesus transforms the valley of Achor into a door of hope. The valley of Achor could also be translated as the *valley of Trouble*. Achan and his family were stoned in this valley after it was revealed that they had taken the forbidden gold from Jericho (Jos. 7:16-26). We can at times feel like we are stuck in the valley of trouble because we are overwhelmed with the problems and challenges of life. But Jesus transforms the valley of trouble into a door of hope, where we can cast our cares upon Him (1 Pet. 5:6-8). When we are together with Jesus, He will always give us a way out of trouble and provide solutions to the problems of life. Jesus Himself is our way out of the valley, no matter how deep we are stuck. *"Then said Jesus unto them again, Verily, verily, I say unto you, I am the door of the sheep. All that ever came before me are thieves and robbers: but the sheep did not hear them. I am the door: by me if any man enters in, he shall be saved, and shall go in and out, and find pasture" (John 10:7-9).* When Jesus opens a door, no man can shut it. He always provides a solution and a way for us that lead to blessing and greater breakthroughs.

## An Everlasting Betrothal in Compassion and Favor

As the bride of Christ, we are now living in an everlasting union with Jesus. This marriage is unbreakable because it rests on His compassion and faithfulness. Hosea describes our union with Jesus with these words: *"I will betroth you to Me forever; Yes, I will betroth you to Me in righteousness and in justice, in favor and in compassion, And I will betroth you to Me in faithfulness. Then you will know the Lord. "And it will come about on that day that I will respond," declares the Lord" (Hos. 2:19-20 NASB).* Our relationship with God is built on the faithfulness of Jesus and our union with Him is filled with the righteousness and justice of God. We have been made the righteousness of God in Christ, and Jesus carried our punishment for sins committed. Therefore, He is just in saving us. His plan for his bride reveals that not only is Jesus merciful in saving us, but *"… that He would be just and the justifier of the one who has faith in Jesus" (Rom. 3:25-26 NASB).* We have access to an abundance of compassion and favor through Jesus Christ. Our identity is found in Christ and as he is, so are we in this world (1 John 4:17). Because of this, we have received a new identity. We are His beloved and favored sons and daughters (Matt 3:16). The fact that we have His favor upon our lives, makes is possible for us to bear fruit that remains (John 15:16).

## We Are His People

As God continues to speak to Hosea, He reveals more of how living with Him in the New Covenant will look like. He does this to reveal His faithfulness and mercy to Hosea:

*I will respond to the heavens, and they will respond to the earth, and the earth will respond to the grain, to the new wine, and to the oil, and they will respond to Jezreel. I will sow her for Myself in the land. I will also have compassion on her who had not obtained compassion, And I will say to those who were not My people, 'You are My people!' And they will say, 'You are my God' (Hos. 2:21-23 NASB).*

We are now His people and Jesus is our promised land. This is a land where the rain of the Spirit is falling, bringing forth a rich harvest every year. The promised land produces an abundance of the wine and oil of the Holy Spirit as well. This promised land has now become ours through our union with Jesus. The fruit and harvest of the promised land is our inheritance. Jesus truly is a faithful Bridegroom!

- Set aside 20-30 minutes for prayer. Ask the Holy Spirit to reveal the faithfulness of Jesus to you. Ask Him to remind you of how Jesus has been faithful to you when you have failed or made mistakes. Write down what He reveals to you.

- Look at the story of your life through the mercy and faithfulness of Jesus Christ. How does your personal history change when you look at it as a testimony of His faithfulness?

- In this chapter, I wrote about the prophet Hosea as an example of God's faithfulness. There are many other examples of His faithful love within the Scriptures. Find two or three more examples of His faithfulness from the Bible. Read their stories and ask the Holy Spirit to give deeper insight on the faithfulness of God from these examples.

- We all know people who struggle to remain in the will of God, or who have backslidden. Take two or three such people in prayer to God and ask Him to bring them back into fellowship with Him. Jesus remains faithful to them even though they have failed Him. His heart is always for the full restoration of all His friends.

# CHAPTER 13: THE HEALING AND RESTORING LOVE OF JESUS CHRIST

In the previous chapter we studied the story of Hosea. His life embodied the faithful love of Jesus. To have personal experience of the faithfulness of Jesus, brings healing and restoration to our deepest wounds. We might be hurt because of our bad choices, or by the abandonment and rejection we have suffered from others. But the Father is faithful to heal our hearts when we come to Him. In this chapter, we will take a deeper look at the healing love of Jesus Christ. His love is powerful and it restores every broken heart. We start by returning to the book of Hosea:

*Come, let's return to the Lord. For He has torn us, but He will heal us; He has wounded us, but He will bandage us. "He will revive us after two days; He will raise us up on the third day, that we may live before Him. "So let's learn, let's press on to know the Lord. His appearance is as sure as the dawn; And He will come to us like the rain, As the spring rain waters the earth (Hos. 6:1-3 NASB).*

When Hosea is speaking about how God has torn us, he does not imply that God was the one who caused the damage within His people. He didn't intentionally leave them brokenhearted. The theme of the book of Hosea is God's faithfulness to an unfaithful people. God always wanted a faithful covenant relationship with His people, but they could still choose to go their own way. They had the freedom to do so because God will not violate the choices of His people.

If we want to go our own way to engage with illegitimate lovers, we have the freedom to do that. But these relationships will cause a lot of harm and destruction in our lives. The prophecy above is speaking about this reality. The damage happened because God permitted the people to walk away from Him, but that does not mean that He was the cause of their pain. They inflicted it upon themselves by their foolish choices. The good news is that they could make a better choice by returning to God whenever they want to. God has promised to heal their hearts by restoring them back to life again. That's His heart toward us as well. The Father longs to heal His people from the wounds of sin.

## The Lord Our Healer

Jesus longs for us to be healed because He is our Healer. He is the Shepherd of our soul. God revealed Himself as our healer when Israel had passed through the Red Sea: *"If you will listen carefully to the voice of the Lord your God, and do what is right in His sight, and listen to His commandments, and keep all His statutes, I will put none of the diseases on you which I have put on the Egyptians; for I, the Lord, am your healer" (Exod. 15:26 NASB).* Jesus is the Lord our healer and the Father is the best physician in the universe. By abiding in His loving presence, we will find healing for our hearts, and our soul will find new life and renewal in Him.

## Jesus Is Resurrection and Life for Our Soul

Hosea also mentioned that we would be raised back to life again. Jesus is Resurrection and Life to us, which is being alluded to by the proclamation that we would be raised on the third day. This prophecy points toward the coming resurrection of Jesus. As we know, Jesus was resurrected on the third day, but this is a promise to us as well. When we come to Jesus, He will revive and renew our spirits by imparting new life to us. We never have to search for revival or renewal. We just need to spend time in the secret place with Jesus, and we will be revived and renewed (Isa. 40:28-31). He will come upon us like the rain, showering us with His healing love.

**The Day of Healing and Restoration Is Here!**

Jesus longs for His bride to be healed and restored. The prophet Isaiah prophesied of a time when this would become reality, a day in which the healing of His people would take place: *"The moon will shine like the sun, and the sunlight will be seven times brighter, like the light of seven full days, when the Lord binds up the bruises of his people and heals the wounds he inflicted"* (Isa. 30:26 NIV). This time is not going to come far off in the future. Isaiah speaks about our day since this prophecy is talking about the New Covenant. *"'In the time of my favor I heard you, and in the day of salvation I helped you.' I tell you, now is the time of God's favor, now is the day of salvation"* (2 Cor. 6:2 NIV). We are now living in a time when we can come to the Father to find healing from the wounds within our hearts.

## Jesus Is the True Shepherd and Loving Guardian of Our Soul

Jesus released rivers of healing love through the cross and by His wounds we have been made whole. We no longer need to chase healing or strive to find freedom. Healing and restoration are our inheritance in Christ. When Jesus went to the cross, He carried our pain and brokenness with Him, nailing it to the cross to provide healing for His bride. *"Our instant healing flowed from his wounding. You were like sheep that continually wandered away, but now you have returned to the true Shepherd of your lives the kind Guardian who lovingly watches over your souls"* (1 Pet. 2:24-25 TPT). Jesus loves us so much that He became one with our pain and brokenness. In exchange, He gave us His wholeness and peace. Jesus wants to lead us into wholeness because He is our true Shepherd, who watches over us in grace and lovingkindness. Jesus cares so deeply about us that He became one with our pain to provide healing for us. This reveals what a humble and loving Bridegroom and friend we have in Jesus.

Jesus is not only interested in fixing us, but our pain matters so much to Him that He is personally walking with us through our process of healing. He leads us into wholeness through a process where He restores us into His image. This takes time, but Jesus will not stop His work within our hearts, until all broken areas have been fully healed and restored. *"The LORD is my shepherd; I shall not want. He maketh me to lie down in green pastures: He leadeth me beside the still waters. He restoreth my soul: He leadeth me in the paths of righteousness for his name's sake" (Ps. 23:1-3).* The ministry of Jesus as our Shepherd reveals the healing love of the Father in a powerful way.

## The Religious Spirit Is a Counterfeit Shepherd

Jesus is our loving shepherd and counselor who leads us into freedom and restoration. Since Satan wants to steal and oppress the Lord's sheep, there is a demonic counterfeit to this aspect of Jesus' ministry. Satan wants to raise up false shepherds whose ministry harms the bride. This counterfeit is the religious spirit who shepherds through religion and legalism. It is important to point out that when speaking of these false shepherds, I am not referring to leaders in the body of Christ. I am speaking of the religious spirit, who operates in a legalistic form of shepherding based on religious rules. This spirit will at times operate through leaders within the church, but people are never our enemy (Eph. 6:12). We can easily discern when Jesus is shepherding us, since He will never lead us by legalistic means, but through grace and a sacrificial love that always reveals the heart of the Father. The religious spirit uses legalism and guilt to drive people. By our motivation for ministry, we can detect what manner of spirit we move in. Our ministry needs to be motivated by the heart of the Father and the love of Jesus Christ.

## The Ministry of the Religious Spirit

Ezekiel gives a warning about the ministry of the religious spirit, which contrasts religious ministry to the ministry of Jesus as our good Shepherd: *"Woe, shepherds of Israel who have been feeding themselves! Should the shepherds not feed the flock? You eat the fat and clothe yourselves with the wool, you slaughter the fat sheep without feeding the flock"* (Ezek. 34:2-3 NASB).  Jesus leads and shepherds His people by laying down His own life for our sake. In the New Covenant, we get all the blessings and benefits of being under the leadership of Jesus. Religious shepherds turn this principle upside down. They shepherd by demanding that we lay down our lives for them, so that they get all the benefits of our religious sacrifices. No one can live with that type of pressure for long. It is possible to create good results short-term by leading like that, but the fruit will always be the same in the end. The bride of Jesus Christ will be left broken, oppressed and confused.

## My Experience with the Religious Spirit

I have had encounters with the religious spirit several times in my ministry. I must deal with it regularly while ministering in churches and at conferences. But now I'm mature enough to handle these confrontations. It was much harder when I was a new believer and came under its influence. I was badly wounded by religion for a couple of years. My breakthrough came when I encountered the heart of the Father and received His loving comfort. I realized that Jesus is nothing like the religious spirit, and knowing who He really is, has set me free. The only antidote to religion and legalism is a revelation of the love of the Father and the New Covenant. Experiencing His loving embrace will make us lose our appetite for religion quickly!

**Religious Shepherds and the Wounding of the Bride**

As Ezekiel continues his prophetic preaching, he addresses the fruit of being ensnared by religious spirit. *"You have not taken care of the weak. You have not tended the sick or bound up the injured. You have not gone looking for those who have wandered away and are lost. Instead, you have ruled them with harshness and cruelty" (Ezek. 34:4 NLT).* We find several bad fruits of being under the oppression of a religious spirit listed within this passage. These fruits will appear wherever the religious spirit has built a stronghold. We can summarize the bad fruit of religious ministry like this:

- *The weak will not be strengthened.*
- *The sick will not get healed.*
- *The broken will not be restored.*
- *The scattered will not be brought back.*
- *The bride of Christ will be dominated and oppressed.*

Being under the leadership of religion and legalistic shepherds will leave the Lord's sheep scattered and defeated. They will then become an easy prey for the enemy lurking in the field: *"So my sheep have been scattered without a shepherd, and they are easy prey for any wild animal. They have wandered through all the mountains and all the hills, across the face of the earth, yet no one has gone to search for them" (Ezek. 34:4-6 NLT).*

**Jesus Rescues and Restores His Defeated People**

Jesus Himself will respond to the abuse and oppression that His people have suffered from the religious spirit. He promises to search for them and to rescue them from their lost and defeated state. *"For the Lord God says this: "Behold, I Myself will search for My sheep and look after them. As a shepherd cares for his flock on a day when he is among his scattered sheep, so I will care for My sheep and will rescue them from all the places where they were scattered on a cloudy and gloomy day" (Ezek. 34:11-12 NASB).* The *"cloudy and gloomy day"* speaks of a season where the daylight is blocked by the clouds, making it hard to see clearly. This represents a season when revelation is lacking. The only way for the bride of Christ to be attracted to religion, is if she has not seen the beauty of Jesus and the glory of the New Covenant. Religion will always leave us in a scattered and disillusioned state. The good news is that Jesus promises to rescue His bride from the oppression of the religious spirit. He will heal and restore her from every wound caused by legalism. Jesus Himself is bringing his bride back to His pastures of healing and peace.

*I will bring them out from the peoples and gather them from the countries and bring them to their own land; and I will feed them on the mountains of Israel, by the streams, and in all the inhabited places of the land. I will feed them in a good pasture, and their grazing place will be on the mountain heights of Israel (Ezek. 34:13-14 NASB).*

Jesus delivers from religious yokes and leads us into the rest of faith where we can feed on the gospel of grace (Ezek. 34:14). The gospel brings healing to the deepest places of our hearts by revealing the heart of the Father and the finished work of Jesus Christ. As we listen to His voice, we will be healed and restored: *"I will search for my lost ones who strayed away, and I will bring them safely home again. I will bandage the injured and strengthen the weak. But I will destroy those who are fat and powerful. I will feed them, yes—feed them justice" (Ezek. 34:15-16 NLT).* Within this prophecy, we can clearly see how the healing love of Jesus flows from His present-day ministry as our good Shepherd. Before, we saw the devastating results of being led by the religious spirit. The fruits of being led by Jesus Christ, the true Shepherd of our souls, are:

- *We will find rest for our souls.*
- *The scattered will be led home to the Father.*
- *The broken will be healed.*
- *The weak will be strengthened.*
- *The religious spirit will be cast out and all its legalistic teachings will be eliminated.*

## The Religious Spirit Will Be Driven Out!

The *fat and powerful* refers to the religious spirit and its legalistic teachings (Ezek. 34:16). These will be driven out from among our midst as we get a deeper revelation of the gospel of Jesus Christ. We break the stronghold of religion by a clear preaching of the gospel of grace and through prayer and intercession. We have received a clear mandate from Jesus to drive out religion and its legalistic teachings from our midst. We then need to replace it by inviting Jesus to take His rightful place as our good Shepherd. Jesus uses the picture of the shepherd when speaking of His own ministry, several times throughout the Scriptures. The ministry of the Shepherd brings healing to the bride of Christ.

## Jesus Is the Good Shepherd

Only a shepherd who serves through self-giving love can create an environment of healing and safety for the people. Jesus is the ultimate example of how to serve in this way. As we have seen, Jesus relates to us through sacrificial and selfless love. He has no hidden plan or selfish agendas in His dealings with us. His only motive is the wellbeing of His bride. *"I am the Good Shepherd who lays down my life as a sacrifice for the sheep"* (John 10:11 TPT). Since Jesus always lays down His life to serve us, the atmosphere and culture He creates is one of healing and safety. This kind of love heals every hurt and delivers from every wound. *"He sent his word, and healed them, and delivered them from their destructions"*

*(Ps. 107:20)*. The Father has an intense love for His Son because Jesus sacrificed Himself to bring the Father's lost children home. This moves the Father in a deep way. The Father is fulfilling the desire of Jesus, by giving Him a bride. Jesus fulfills the dream of the Father, by bringing His lost children back home. *"The Father has an intense love for me because I freely give my own life—to raise it up again. I surrender my own life, and no one has the power to take my life from me. I have the authority to lay it down and the power to take it back again. This is the destiny my Father has set before me"* (John 10:17-18 TPT).

## Jesus Became One with Our Pain

Jesus demonstrated what it really means to be a good shepherd by becoming one with our suffering and brokenness on the cross. Isaiah calls Jesus a man of sorrows because He became one with our pain and wounds. *"He is despised and rejected of men; a man of sorrows, and acquainted with grief: and we hid as it were our faces from him; he was despised, and we esteemed him not"* (Isa. 53:3). Jesus did this to restore us back into His image. Isaiah is prophesying about the redemptive work of Jesus here. It is impossible to fully understand the amount of pain that Jesus experienced on the cross, but when we catch a glimpse of the love it reveals, our hearts will be healed from rejection and abandonment. *"But He was pierced for our offenses, He was crushed for our wrongdoings; the punishment for our well-being was laid upon Him, and by His wounds we are healed* (Isa. 53:4-5 NASB). Jesus took our punishment upon Himself to give us His peace and He absorbed our wounds to make us whole again. Jesus provided complete healing for all the pain that we have ever suffered. He did that by taking it all upon Himself, nailing it to the cross once and for all.

## The Reward of His Suffering

Jesus endured the cross because of the reward that was set before Him. Through His finished work, the Father's plan now prospers and Jesus will see the fruit of His suffering and be satisfied: *"But it was the Lord's good plan to crush him and cause him grief. Yet when his life is made an offering for sin, he will have many descendants. He will enjoy a long life, and the Lord's good plan will prosper in his hands (Isa. 53:10 NLT).* Through the sacrifice of Jesus, the Father brings His lost children home and His dream of having a big family is now being fulfilled. What Jesus accomplished on the cross is so far reaching that even in eternity, we will keep on discovering new aspects of His redemptive work. Even though the suffering was horrifying, Jesus is rejoicing because He enjoys the glorious fruit of His suffering: *"When he sees all that is accomplished by his anguish, he will be satisfied"* (Isa. 53:11 NLT).

## There Is Healing in His Presence

Just like it is impossible to jump into the water without getting wet, so it is impossible to be in the presence of the Jesus Christ without being healed. Healing for the brokenhearted is always found through intimacy with God. Malachi makes this prophetic statement concerning Jesus: *"But unto you that fear my name shall the Sun of righteousness arise with healing in his wings; and ye shall go forth, and grow up as calves of the stall"* (Mal. 4:2). As we abide in the presence of Jesus, we will find healing and refreshing for our souls. Sometimes we have made inner healing a complicated issue that is reserved for experts only, but the truth is that healing ministry is for every believer. We are all called to bring healing to the wounded and to restore the fallen (Gal 6:1-2). The most important thing when ministering healing, is to bring people into His presence, because it is there that we will find healing that lasts. This is true when it comes to our healing as well. In His presence, we find an endless source of comfort, encouragement and peace.

## Jesus and His Bride Bring Healing to the Nations

We find healing in the presence of the Bridegroom and as we are being restored, our past brokenness loses its power to define who we are. The bride of Christ is not forsaken and barren. We have not been left desolate and irrelevant in the desert. We are now being restored into our true bridal identity and Jesus will bring healing to the nations through us. *"And he that overcometh, and keepeth my works unto the end, to him will I give power over the nations: and he shall rule them with a rod of iron; as the vessels of a potter shall they be broken to shivers: even as I received of my Father"* (*Rev. 2:26-27*). Remember that Jesus shepherds through sacrificial love and that He rules with humility and grace. The bride of Christ will shepherd the nations together with Him. As we are arising into that sphere of authority, the nations will be healed as the rivers of living waters flow through us. The nations will once again eat from the tree of life through the ministry of the body of Christ (Rev. 22:1-2). We are being healed and restored through the love of Christ, but that love is now flowing through us as well, bringing healing and revival to the nations.

# Activations

- Set aside 20-30 minutes for prayer. Ask the Holy Spirit to reveal more of the healing love of Jesus to you, and to show you what it means that Jesus is the Shepherd of your soul. Write down the revelation you receive.

- Invite Jesus to bring healing to broken areas of your life. Ask Him to shepherd your soul into wholeness and to restore every broken place within your heart.

- In this chapter we studied Ezekiel chapter thirty-four to see the difference between the religious spirit and Jesus. Read it again together with the Holy Spirit. Ask Him for more revelation and write down what He shows you.

- Invite Jesus to reveal Himself as the Good Shepherd through you and ask Him to minister healing to broken people through you. You are called to be a healer of broken hearts!

# CHAPTER 14: LOVE THAT SANCTIFIES AND TRANSFORMS

In the previous chapter, we studied how Jesus is the Shepherd and Healer of our soul. Another important characteristic of Jesus that is closely associated to Him being our Healer, is that Jesus is our sanctification. He is the one who purifies and sanctifies His people: *"Surely My Sabbaths you shall keep, for it is a sign between Me and you throughout your generations, that you may know that I am the Lord who sanctifies you" (Exod. 31:13 NKJV).* In a previous chapter of this book, we saw how we have been made perfect and sanctified through the cross. Jesus is currently bringing us through a process of transformation through which He causes our lifestyle to match our identity. This is where our relationship with God comes in. It is by living in fellowship with Jesus that we are being transformed. We are perfect while being perfected into His image. We can be fully confident that Jesus will not stop until His work within us is fully done. *"…being confident of this very thing, that he which hath begun a good work in you will perform it until the day of Jesus Christ" (Phil. 1:6).* This is a work of grace, which can often be a bit challenging for us, even to the point of leaving us with a limp. We find a very good example of a limping man of God in Jacob. He became a very different man after His encounter with the Lord.

## Jacob Wrestles with God

Jacob had been a schemer and deceiver all his life, trying to get ahead through deception and by cheating whomever he could take advantage of (See Jacob's story in Genesis chapters 25-49). The name Jacob means *heel-grabber* and *supplanter*. That name describes his character because he was a chronical deceiver. This character was so cemented within him that it had become his identity. But finally, the night had arrived when his old ways of deception and trickery was to no avail. God confronted Jacob up close and personal, wrestling with him all night to break him free from this false self. God knew that for Jacob to walk in his destiny as a father of God's people, his supplanting and deceiving nature needed to die.

Jacob had an intense encounter with God that night: *"Then Jacob was left alone, and a man wrestled with him until daybreak. When the man saw that he had not prevailed against him, he touched the socket of Jacob's hip; and the socket of Jacob's hip was dislocated while he wrestled with him"* (Gen. 32:24-25 NASB). This mysterious man could not defeat Jacob by wrestling him, so he dislocated Jacob's hip. The hip is a symbol of the strength of man, and dislocating it became an outward sign of inner brokenness. Jacob walked with a limp for the rest of his life, but from that moment he was a different man. We will have similar experiences to this, where we encounter God and wrestle with Him. Jesus confronts us to break our trust in the flesh and to deliver us from the things that hinder us from walking in our bridal identity. He is challenging us to say yes to His dealings, by living in humble abandonment before our heavenly Father. To do that, our old fleshly ways must be killed off and die. Jesus is our sanctification and He will handle this process personally. Paul writes: *"But of him are ye in Christ Jesus, who of God is made unto us wisdom, and righteousness, and sanctification, and redemption: that, according as it is written, He that glorieth, let him glory in the Lord"* (1 Cor. 1:30-31). In the New Covenant, Jesus Himself sanctifies His people, and we are being transformed as we give Him permission to change our lives.

## Jacob Becomes Israel

As Jacob continues His battle with the mysterious wrestler, dawn was breaking in. But Jacob refuses to let the man go without first blessing him:

*Then he said, "Let me go, for the dawn is breaking." But he said, "I will not let you go unless you bless me." So he said to him, "What is your name?" And he said, "Jacob." Then he said, "Your name shall no longer be Jacob, but Israel; for you have contended with God and with men, and have prevailed" (Gen 32:26- 28 NASB).*

The man did not bless Jacob immediately. Instead, He asked Jacob what his name was. There was a reason for this. The real question for Jacob to answer was this one: "Jacob, are you finally ready to be honest and tell me who you really are? Are we done with the lies and deceptions yet"? When Jacob answered by saying his name, he admitted who he really was. A deceiver and a supplanter, who had learned to get ahead in life by deception and lies. Truth and honesty are always a point of connection with God and transformation always start by being truthful with the issues of our hearts. When we live authentically with Jesus in this way, His grace brings deep transformation, even if the process sometimes can be both challenging and painful.

## A Change of Names

*And Jacob asked him and said, "Please tell me your name." But he said, "Why is it that you ask my name?" And he blessed him there. So Jacob named the place Peniel, for he said, "I have seen God face to face, yet my life has been spared" (Gen. 32:29-30 NASB).* The mysterious man blessed Jacob and changed his name to Israel. Names in the Bible carry prophetic significance. They were not given randomly, but they were meant to be a declaration of destiny in God. When

Jacob's named was changed, the Lord revealed his real identity. Jacob had now been transformed into Israel. The supplanter had now become a ruler. The prophecy that had been spoken over Jacob long ago finally started to be fulfilled: *"Two nations are in your womb; And two peoples will be separated from your body; And one people will be stronger than the other; And the older will serve the younger" (Gen. 25:23 NASB).* Jacob was now finally ready to stop his deceptive games and allow God to fulfill His promises.

## Jesus Wrestles with Us

The man wrestling with Jacob was not an ordinary man. Jacob had wrestled with God Himself and had seen Him face to face! This mysterious wrestler was Jesus Himself. This is yet another one of Jesus' appearances in the Old Testament. Of course, Jesus could easily have defeated Jacob in an instant, but Jesus rules with humility and grace. He never uses excessive force or control against His people. This was not a competition of strength, but God wanted to expose Jacob's heart to reveal that Jacob couldn't win this fight through deception. The only way forward was to die to his old scheming character. Jacob the deceiver died that night. Instead, Israel the ruler with God was born. Even though Jacob walked with a limp for the rest of his life he had finally found his strength in God.

## The Discipline of God

Jacob's encounter with God is a very good example of how Jesus transforms us. He brings us into situations where our hearts are exposed. He then wrestles with us until we realize that only by dying to our old ways can we prevail with God. The old lifestyle must be crucified for the purposes of God to come to pass in our lives. *"My son, do not make light of the Lord's discipline, and do not lose heart when he rebukes you, because the Lord disciplines the one he loves, and he chastens everyone he accepts as his son" (Hebr. 12:5-6 NIV).* The discipline of the Lord is a sign of legitimate sonship (Hebr. 12:8). Even though the discipline of the Lord can be a bit painful at times, the reward of being disciplined makes it worth enduring the pain. *"No discipline seems pleasant at the time, but painful. Later on, however, it produces a harvest of righteousness and peace for those who have been trained by it" (Hebr. 12:11 NIV).* The story of Jacob illustrates what the sanctifying work of God can look like. Jesus is our sanctification and He handles the work of transformation in our lives personally. Being disciplined by God does not mean that He punishes us, but that He wants to prune us so that we can reach our full potential in Christ.

## The Sanctifying Grace of God

Since the kingdom of God operates through humility and self-giving love, Jesus deals with us in gentleness and humility. We are transformed by a work of His grace. The grace of God is His unmerited favor and goodwill toward us, but it is also His divine ability that empowers us to be and do whatever He has called us to be and do. This is the reason Paul writes:

*For the grace of God that bringeth salvation hath appeared to all men, teaching us that, denying ungodliness and worldly lusts, we should live soberly, righteously, and godly, in this present world (Tit. 2:11-12).*

Jesus usually leads in a very gentle way. But sometimes He must be a bit firmer with us, like he was with Jacob. Jesus will at times address the motives of our heart, but we must remember that He never dominates or controls us. This is the reason that there are a lot of things going on within the body of Christ that are not according to His will. We have freedom to respond to Him, or to choose our own ways instead, but we will have to live with the fruit of our choices.

The grace of God teaches us to live in sanctification by inviting us into a relationship with Jesus, where His love transforms our heart so that we can reflect Him. Jesus longs for a bride that freely responds to His transforming work. When we give Him access to new areas of our lives, the Holy Spirit starts a transforming process in these areas to make us look like Jesus. This is how grace teaches us to deny ungodliness and worldly desires.

## Being Transformed from Glory to Glory

As we respond to the call to grow in intimacy with Jesus, our revelation of Him will grow deeper as well. When we abide in His presence, that which is incompatible with His nature will be broken in our lives. This process continues until we are fully conformed into the image of Jesus. *"Now the Lord is the Spirit, and where the Spirit of the Lord is, there is freedom. But we all, with unveiled faces, looking as in a mirror at the glory of the Lord, are being transformed into the same image from glory to glory, just as from the Lord, the Spirit"* (2 Cor. 3:17-18 NASB). Our only responsibility in this process is to keep our hearts open to Him, saying yes to His transforming work in our lives. We can delay this process by not cooperating with the work of the Holy Spirit, but His goal for our lives will not change. It will only take a little bit longer for His plan to be accomplished.

I have always been very fascinated by this process and I enjoy following people on their journey of transformation with Jesus. Watching how Jesus saves and transforms a person, loving them into wholeness and holiness is a very powerful experience. Jesus brings transformation when we give Him access to our hearts. We are invited to do that as soon as an issue is brought into the light. He will put us in situations and relationships where the issues of our heart surface again and again, until we are ready to give them to Him. When we do that, a process of purification and deliverance will begin. This is how Jesus sanctifies His people.

## Peter Refuses to Listen to Jesus

Peter was the most self-confident of the twelve disciples. He had walked on water; he had a revelation that Jesus was the Messiah. He was even brave enough to take on a whole legion of soldiers by himself. Yet, Peter was struggling with one big weakness that continually caused him to stumble. That weakness was his pride and confidence in his own abilities. This made him an easy target for Satan. The night that Jesus was betrayed, He warned Peter about the coming trial: *"Simon, Simon! Indeed, Satan has asked for you, that he may sift you as wheat. But I have prayed for you, that your faith should not fail; and when you have returned to Me, strengthen your brethren" (Luke 22:31-32 NKJV).* When Jesus speaks a word of warning to us, it is a good idea to pay attention.

But Peter could not receive this warning because he was blinded by pride and arrogance. *"But he said to Him, "Lord, I am ready to go with You, both to prison and to death. "Then He said, "I tell you, Peter, the rooster shall not crow this day before you will deny three times that you know Me" (Luke 22:33-34 NKJV).* Peter was confident that he could handle this situation better than anyone else, saying that even if all the others would leave, he would remain with Jesus (Matt. 26:33).

## Peter Realizes the Truth about Himself

We know that pride always goes before a fall, and Peter woke up to the truth of this in a brutal way. Due to everything that went on during that night, Peter had forgotten about Jesus' warning and ended up denying Jesus three times. When he denied Jesus for the third time, the rooster crowed. *"And then the Lord turned and looked at Peter. And Peter remembered the word of the Lord, how He had told him, "Before a rooster crows today, you will deny Me three times." And he went out and wept bitterly"* (Luke 22:60-62 NASB). When Jesus looked Peter in the eyes, Peter remembered Jesus' warning and broke down crying.

Remember that the eyes of Jesus are like flames of fire, burning with a passionate love for us. This night, while looking at Peter, the eyes of Jesus was filled with mercy, love and forgiveness. Jesus knew what Peter was going through, but he chose not to intervene. Peter had to experience this failure to be humbled and delivered from his prideful ways. Otherwise, Peter would have become an unbroken and dangerous leader, leading by human strength. In the kingdom of God, only humility and self-giving love works as a motivation for ministry.

## Jesus' Special Greeting to Peter

This was a very dark season for Peter. He had failed Jesus by denying Him three times and even cursing while doing it (Matt. 26:74). But Jesus loved Peter and He had already planned for his restoration. Jesus wanted to make sure that Peter knew that Jesus was still his friend, so the angel told the women visiting the grave of Jesus to give Peter a special greeting: *"But go, tell His disciples and Peter, 'He is going ahead of you to Galilee; there you will see Him, just as He told you"* (Mark 16:7 NASB). I have noticed how Jesus has encouraged me in similar ways when I go through a process of transformation. These processes can be painful, but during the pain, Jesus speaks encouragement and comfort. When Jesus and Peter met at the shore of the sea of Galilee, Jesus restored Peter from each of his three denials, by giving him the opportunity to express his love for Jesus three times.

## Jesus Restores Peter

The process of restoration did not start with Jesus pointing out Peter's failure. He never even mentioned Peter's denial at all. That was not what was important to Jesus here. Instead, Jesus addressed Peter's heart to restore their relationship and the close connection that they used to share. Jesus did that by asking the same simple question three times:

- *Jesus said to Simon Peter, "Simon, son of John, do you love Me more than these" (John 21:15 NASB)?*
- *He said to him again, a second time, "Simon, son of John, do you love Me" (John 21:16 NASB)?*
- *He said to him the third time, "Simon, son of John, do you love Me" (John 21:17 NASB)?*

Jesus knew that Peter loved him, but He also knew that Peter needed to remember that. Self-accusation and guilt had blinded Peter and he needed to be reminded of who he really was. Since Jesus has no shame or condemnation to give, He does not put shame and guilt on fallen and broken disciples. Jesus restores and gives second chances. Peter answered affirmatively to Jesus' questions. Peter was given the opportunity to express his love for Jesus three times, one for each denial. Each time Jesus once again confirmed Peter's calling, affirming that Peter was restored into God's purpose:

- *"Feed My lambs" (John 21:15).*
- *"Feed My sheep" (John 21:16).*
- *"Feed My sheep" (John 21:17).*

Peter came out of this as a new man. He was now a broken and humble man, ready to step into the work Jesus had prepared for him. Peter now knew by experience that he had to trust in Jesus because he was too weak in himself. Peter's human strength was now broken, he was finally ready to listen and to be led by Jesus (John 21:18-19). The glorious fruit of transformation will always be humility and Christlikeness.

## Embracing the Transforming Love of Jesus

The examples mentioned within this chapter shows us how Jesus operates as *the Lord who sanctifies*. That Jesus is our sanctification is not just a judicial truth, but it means that He is personally involved in our transformation. My wife has shared a powerful testimony about this. When she was being asked about the most powerful miracle she has seen in our ministry, she answered that it would probably be the transformation which has taken place in my life. She said that walking with the Lord through some very painful and dark seasons, has transformed me into a much more relaxed and peaceful man. The fruit of transformation is glorious. Therefore, Jesus invites us to embrace transformation by saying yes to His work within our lives.

# Activations

- Set aside 20-30 minutes for prayer. Ask the Holy Spirit to give more revelation on the sanctifying love of Christ, as well as your own process of being transformed. Write down the insights you receive.

- Within this chapter, we have been looking at two very good examples of the transforming love of God from the lives of Jacob and Peter. There are many more such examples to be found in the Bible. Find two or three of them and ask the Holy Spirit to give more revelation on this topic through these examples.

- Have you had your own wrestling match with God like Jacob? Have you had a failure like Peter that the Lord has used to transform your life? Write your own story of spiritual formation with God. You will be encouraged by noticing how much He has already done in your life.

- Take some time in prayer and invite the Holy Spirit to speak into your journey of transformation. What is He working on right now in your life? What has Jesus done to make you more Christlike? What do you want Him to do? Invite Him to show you areas that He wants to work on and ask Him to transform these specific areas.

# CHAPTER 15: A BLESSED BRIDE

The bride of Christ has been blessed with all the riches of heaven. These blessings are our inheritance through Jesus Christ (Eph. 1:3). But when our identity has been shaped by a broken past, it can sometimes feel like we are stuck in defeat and frustration. If that happens, our past can become a curse that it seems almost impossible to break free from. I certainly felt like that for a long time. I had developed a very broken view of myself, thinking that I could never find a way out of the pain of the past. I firmly believed that I was conditioned to failure and that I had been set up to be a loser in life. This became a self-fulfilling prophecy that caused a lot of frustration and pain. Since I believed that I would fail at the things I wanted to accomplish in life, accepting failure and quitting became my lifestyle. My real breakthrough came as I realized that through Jesus, every curse is dissolved and that the cycle of failure had been broken. I started to see that through Jesus Christ, I had become destined to overcome every obstacle, fulfilling my calling by living a life that bears fruit (John 15:16). This is our destiny as the bride of Christ!

## The Original Blessing

The story of mankind did not start with the fall of Adam and Eve. It started with a blessing, which is commonly referred to as the original blessing. God spoke this blessing over humanity when He created Adam. This happened before Adam and Eve fell into sin. The biblical principle is that blessing always come before the curse and the blessing will prevail after the curse is dissolved:

*So God created man in His own image, in the image of God He created him; male and female He created them. God blessed them; and God said to them, "Be fruitful and multiply, and fill the earth, and subdue it; and rule over the fish of the sea and over the birds of the sky and over every living thing that moves on the earth" (Gen. 1:28 NASB).*

This blessing has never been revoked and through Christ we are now able to live in the fullness of it. We have been blessed with fruitfulness and multiplication, causing us to have dominion over the earth because we are God's ambassadors here. As we walk with God, we can expect God to bless us with favor and increase in all our ways. This will cause the work of our hands to prosper. When Adam and Eve fell into sin, the destructive forces of sin and death were released upon the earth and man came under a curse (Gen. 3:14-19, Rom. 5:12). The good news is that this curse has been broken through Christ. Now we have access to the original blessing once again.

### Every Curse Is Broken in Christ

*Christ redeemed us from the curse of the law by becoming a curse for us, for it is written: "Cursed is everyone who is hung on a pole." He redeemed us in order that the blessing given to Abraham might come to the Gentiles through Christ Jesus, so that by faith we might receive the promise of the Spirit (Gal. 3:13-14 NIV).*

I have observed that some believers become a bit paranoid when it comes to curses, especially generational curses, or the type of curses caused by witchcraft. Since Jesus became a curse for us, there is no need for us to be afraid anymore. These curses have been broken and dissolved. The Message translates these verses like this: *"Christ redeemed us from that self-defeating, cursed life by absorbing it completely into himself. Do you remember the Scripture that says, "Cursed is everyone who hangs on a tree"? That is what happened when Jesus was nailed to the cross: He became a curse, and at the same time dissolved the curse (Gal. 3:13-14 The Message).* Because Jesus did this, we have now received the full blessing of heaven.

This is our new identity. We have been made co-heirs with Jesus Christ. The only way for us to come under a curse today, is by a lack of revelation of the blessing in the New Covenant. Satan can then use ignorance to deceive us into accepting oppression.

The truth is that we are the blessed bride of Jesus Christ, and the people whom God has blessed cannot be cursed. Let's look at an event from the book of Numbers that makes this clear.

## Balaam Was Requested to Curse God's People

While Israel was journeying through the desert, they sometimes were attacked by the inhabitants of the land and had to engage in battles. Because the blessing of God was upon them, they were victorious whenever they went to war. As they came into the territory of Moab, Balak, the Moabite king, became very nervous. He knew that they were too strong for him to defeat in outright battle. So Balak sent for Balaam, asking him to curse the people of Israel (Num. 22:1-6). King Balak thought that if he couldn't defeat Israel in battle, maybe he could win by using witchcraft. God gave Balaam a clear answer to the king's request: *"And God said unto Balaam, thou shalt not go with them; thou shalt not curse the people: for they are blessed" (Num. 22:12).* At first, Balaam listened to God and did not join king Balak to curse Israel. Balak did not give up but sent for Balaam a second time. Balaam denied this request as well, but during the night God spoke to him: *"If the men have come to call you, rise and go with them; but you shall do only the thing that I tell you." So Balaam arose in the morning, saddled his donkey, and went with the leaders of Moab" (Num. 22:20-21 NASB).*

## Balaam's Foolishness

Even though God allowed Balaam to join the leaders back to Moab, He was angry with Balaam for going (Num. 22:21-35). In fact, the angel of the Lord almost killed him. It might appear confusing that God first told Balaam not to travel to Moab, but then changed His mind and allowed Balaam to join the company, while still being angry with him for going. The way God acted in this situation becomes less confusing when we realize that God knew Balaam's heart. He knew that Balaam had set his heart on going and that Balaam wanted King Balak's reward (2 Pet. 2:15, Jude 1:11). Sometimes God will concede and grant us our heart's desire even if it goes against His will, but we will still reap the harvest of our foolishness. God calls the way of Balaam insanity and madness (2 Pet 2:16). Tragically, Balaam ended up dying as a sorcerer because of the greed within his heart (Jos. 13:22). It is much better for us to align our heart with the will of God in obedience, than trying to make Him align with our fallen desires.

### The People of God Cannot Be Cursed

Balaam tried to curse Israel several times, but no curses worked. Balaam could only bless God's people (Num. 23:1-24:25). He realized that his spells were powerless against God's chosen ones. During his first attempt to curse them, Balaam declared: *"No curse can touch Jacob; no magic has any power against Israel. For now it will be said of Jacob, 'What wonders God has done for Israel"* (Num. 23:23 NLT). Each time Balaam tried to manipulate God to curse Israel, he had to bless them instead. They could not be cursed. *"How am I to put a curse on him upon whom God has not put a curse? And how am I to curse him whom the Lord has not cursed"* (Num. 23:8 NASB)?

Balak took Balaam to a high place, from which he attempted to curse Israel a second time. But once again, Balaam had to declare a blessing over them with these words: *"Behold, I have received a command to bless; When He has blessed, I cannot revoke it. "He has not looked at misfortune in Jacob; Nor has He seen trouble in Israel; The Lord his God is with him, And the joyful shout of a king is among them"*

*(Num. 23:20-21 NASB).* Balak tried one last time to make Balaam curse the people of Israel, but it still didn't work. The people of God are uncursable. Instead, Balaam prophesied by declaring a third powerful blessing over Israel. *"Blessed is everyone who blesses you, and cursed is everyone who curses you" (Num. 24:9 NASB).*

The bride of Christ is uncursable. Since the Father has blessed us, no one can successfully curse us. Spells and magic are powerless against the bride of Christ and so is every other type of curse. We are the blessed and favored bride of Christ. Nothing can ever change that! Balaam did not want to bless the people of God, but God made him do it. *"But I was not willing to listen to Balaam. So he had to bless you, and I saved you from his hand" (Jos. 24:10 NASB).*

### Delivered from the Curse of the Law

We have already seen how Jesus has delivered us from the curse of the law (Gal. 3:13-14). The curse of the law is expanded upon in Deuteronomy chapter 28, where the consequences of being under the law is listed. We are going to study these consequences here. Many believers are still experiencing some of the effects of the curse, even though we have already been redeemed from it. When Jesus became a curse for us, He dissolved all consequences of being under the law. It is our inheritance to walk in the full blessing that is ours in Christ. The process of going from curse to blessing takes time, but as we walk with Jesus, these blessings will be released in our lives. Here is a list from Deuteronomy 28, listing the effects of the curse that we have been delivered from:

- ***We have been delivered from a cursed home and living situation. (Deut. 28:16).*** I sometimes minister to people who constantly seem to have some kind of struggle in their home. They feel like a curse rest upon them when it comes to their house and properties. Their home is either torn apart by constant conflict and strife, or there seems to always be some problem with their house and property. But as we have prayed and declared the victory and blessing of Christ over their residence, God has restored their home and blessed it with peace and wholeness once again.

- *We have been delivered from curses concerning our children. (Deut. 28:18, 32).* The curses mentioned here refer to our children being cursed from the womb, and them being taken captive by the enemy. The good news is that these curses are broken and the enemy has no right to our kids anymore. We can now boldly pray and intercede for our kids, knowing that Jesus broke every curse concerning our descendants.

- *We have been delivered from curses concerning our belongings, property, and our work. (Deut. 28:17-19, 30, 33).* Everything that we own, including our work, is protected by the favor and grace of God. Through Jesus all curses in these areas have been broken once and for all. The presence of God surrounds us and everything we own as a shield. He fills our lives with peace.

- *We have been delivered from curses of defeat and slavery. (Deut. 28:20, 25-26, 45-57, 68).* If a person has failed repeatedly in life, it may appear to them that they have been cursed to lose in life. But Jesus Christ broke these curses through the cross and transformed us from sinners into overcomers and conquerors. We have been born again to overcome (Rom. 8:37).

- *We have been delivered from curses of sickness (Deut. 28:21-22, 27-28, 35, 58-62).* Sickness is not a blessing.

When Jesus went to the cross, He carried our sicknesses to provide healing for us. By His stripes we are healed. Jesus has broken the curses of sickness, so that we can be blessed with good health (Isa. 53:4-5).

- *We have been delivered from a closed heaven (Deut. 28:23-24).* Some believers feel like they have lost their connection with God and that they live under a closed heaven. This might be their experience, but it is not their reality anymore. Through Jesus, heaven is always open and we have been blessed with instant access to our Father (John 1:51).

- *We have been delivered from curses of mental torment and oppression (Deut. 28:20, 28-29, 34, 36-37, 43, 65-67).* A lot of people are struggling with mental health issues today. That can certainly feel like a curse, but the good news is that mental torment and oppression is not your inheritance. Jesus wore a crown of thorns as a symbol of a tormented and oppressed mind (Matt. 27:29). He took our mental torment upon Himself on the cross and broke the curse of mental oppression. This means that Jesus is our deliverance from a tormented mind.

- *We have been delivered from the curses of losing our harvest and fruit (Deut. 28:40-42, 51, 63-64).* Some people sow a lot of good seed into the Kingdom of God, but it seems like they are constantly losing out on their harvest. Jesus has broken that curse on the cross so that we can be blessed with an abundant harvest. We have been destined by God to bear fruit that remains (John 15:16).

- ***We have been delivered from curses of debt (Deut. 28:44).*** I meet believers who have been struggling with debt and financial challenges all their life. This is not the will of God. Jesus nailed poverty and debt to the cross, setting us free from every curse concerning our finances. We have now been delivered from the bondage of lack and debt. The Father wants us to prosper in all areas of life, including our finances (Deut. 8:18, 2 Cor. 8:9).

- ***We have been delivered from curses of humiliation (Deut. 28:37, 45-46).*** Sometimes believers describe how they are living in a pattern where they are always humiliated, walked over and taken advantage of. This is not God's will. Jesus broke this curse and has blessed us with favor among the nations. We are called to be the head and not the tail, and to be a light to the nations (Isa. 60:1-5).

Once we realize that these curses have been dissolved and that they have no place in our lives anymore, we can renounce them in prayer. As you have read this list, you might have noticed that some of these curses still seem to be operating in your life. That simply means that your deliverance is soon here. The blessing of God is about to manifest more than ever. It might take some time, but your breakthrough is coming! I enjoy praying and declaring this list over my family to establish our freedom in Christ. But even more, I declare a list of blessings over us. This helps me to stay within a mindset of favor and blessing.

# The Blessing in Deuteronomy 28

Deuteronomy 28 starts by revealing the blessings of obedience to God (Deut. 28:1-2). In the Old Covenant, receiving the blessings of God depended on our obedience. Now, these blessings belong to us because of the vicarious obedience of Jesus Christ. Since Jesus fulfilled the law in our place, these blessings are now our inheritance. We are blessed with the fruit of His obedience (Matt. 5:17-18). Here is a list of twelve powerful blessings that we find in Deuteronomy 28. This list provides a good example of how Jesus has blessed every area of our lives. You can use this list for prayer and as declarations of the Father's favor upon your life:

1. *Our home and living situation are blessed (Deut. 28:2-3).* Our homes were never meant to be a place of stress, dysfunction or lack. Jesus is the Prince of peace and He wants our homes to be blessed with peace, joy and righteousness. Jesus wants to fill our living situation with divine harmony. Because of this, we can boldly declare the blessing and peace of God upon our home and residence.

2. *Our children are blessed by God (Deut. 28:4).* We can be certain that the blessing of God follows our children and descendants everywhere. As a result of us being united with Christ, generational blessings will rest on our children and descendants for many generations. They will be disciples of Jesus and their lives will be surrounded by the peace of the Father. It might not look like that at this moment, but God is working on their heart right now (Deut. 7:13, Isa. 44:3, 54:13).

3.  *Our investment and all the work of our hands are blessed (Deut. 28:4-5).* We have been given ability to create wealth. The favor of God is upon us in our work, opening new doors for us so that the work of our hands prospers (Deut. 8:18). The marketplace is the most important mission field of our day, and we can always count on the favor of God operating on our behalf at our work, so that we can reach our co-workers with the gospel.

4.  *Whatever we come into is blessed (Deut. 28:6).* When we enter a new season in life we are blessed. Whether this season involves beginning at a new job, getting married or becoming a parent, we come into every season blessed by God. Whenever we enter a new season of life, we walk in the blessing of God. Entering a new phase in life can feel intimidating but knowing that our coming in is blessed will help us to enter all phases of life with a humble boldness and confidence.

5.  *Whatever we come out of is blessed (Deut. 28:6).* Whenever a season in our life is over, our Father has declared our coming out of it to be fully blessed. We should never accept to come out of any season or stage in life broken and defeated. God wants us to come out of our old seasons and times blessed and fruitful.

6.  *We have been blessed with victory over the enemy, who will flee from us (Deut. 28:7).* The blessing of God causes the enemy to flee. We are blessed with victory in all spiritual warfare. When it seems like we are in a losing battle, it just means that we have

not seen the end of it yet. As we stand firm in our identity in Christ, the devil must flee from us. We are born again to win (Luke 10:17-19)!

7. *The works of our hands are blessed (Deut. 28:8).* Jesus loves creativity, and when we create with our hands, our work and creativity will be blessed with the favor of God. Whether we are working in some type of ministry or in the marketplace, the works of our hands are blessed by God. This is our inheritance as His beloved and favored children. We can always expect the works of our hands to be anointed with favor and grace (Ps. 90:16-17, Prov. 22:29).

8. *Our God-given land is blessed (Deut. 28:8).* This blessing applies both to the natural as well as to the spiritual land that we have received from God. Our land is blessed with increase and fruitfulness. We can claim this blessing for the land that we own in this world, as well as the spiritual territory that God has given to us. What we have received by grace is always protected and blessed by the favor of God!

9. *We are blessed with favor and grace among the nations (Deut. 28:9-10).* We have already seen how we are called to disciple the nations and release healing to them together with Jesus Christ. We can't do this in our own strength, but we are blessed with great favor and open doors among the nations. As Jesus is being revealed through His bride, all nations will be transformed by the power of the gospel (Isa. 60:1-7).

10. ***We are blessed with prosperity in everything that we own and produce (Deut. 28:11-12).*** Everything that we own is blessed by God, and we can expect it to produce a rich harvest for us, which will increase in value over time. We need to know our properties are blessed to increase. The blessing of the Father causes us to prosper in all things (2 Cor. 8:9)!

11. ***We are blessed to rule and reign in life (Deut. 28:13).*** We have been blessed with royal authority in Christ. We are seated in heavenly places together with Him. That means that we are ruling together with the King of kings. Life was never meant to rule us, leaving us powerless and passive. We are destined to rule in life while experiencing the fullness of God's blessings in Jesus Christ (Rom. 5:17)!

12. ***We are blessed to be over and not beneath (Deut. 28:13).*** As children of God, we have been destined to live above every circumstance. Since we are united with Christ, we are blessed to be over every situation we face in life (Eph. 1:18-23, 2:6). The blessing of God causes all things to work for our good, so that we can bear lasting fruit.

I mentioned how I used to believe that I was born to lose. I felt powerless to make positive changes in my life. But that is a lie. We have been seated with Christ in heavenly places, far above every principality and power. We have been called to reign in life with Christ through his abundant grace. This will cause us to live with a daily expectancy of favor and increase. That is exactly what God wants!

## We Are Blessed

*"Blessed be the God and Father of our Lord Jesus Christ, who hath blessed us with all spiritual blessings in heavenly places in Christ"* *(Eph. 1:3).* All spiritual blessings are already ours in Christ, which means that we have been given unfathomable spiritual riches. It will take all eternity to explore all the riches that is ours through Jesus. We carry more of God's favor than we can handle and we have been destined for a life of blessing and breakthrough. Since God is with us, it is normal for us to have favor with people and to succeed in what we are doing. We are an overcoming bride, who is carrying a destiny to influence and transform this world by revealing Jesus to the nations.

## The Blessing of Aaron

Probably the most famous blessing in the whole Bible is the high priestly blessing, which is also called the Aaronite blessing. The high priest was commanded by God to bless the people of Israel by declaring these words over them: *"The Lord bless you and keep you; the Lord make his face shine on you and be gracious to you; the Lord turn his face toward you and give you peace. So they will put my name on the Israelites, and I will bless them"* *(Num. 6:24-26 NIV).* Jesus Christ is our eternal High Priest and this blessing belongs to us. We live in the reality of this blessing right now. The face of Jesus shines upon us and He is gracious to us. His face is turned towards us and He has blessed us with peace. We no longer need to ask Him to bless us, because He has already given all spiritual blessings in Christ. In the New Covenant, we are living from a place of already being blessed. Knowing this gives us security and confidence in knowing that the blessing of God operates on our behalf. We can boldly make this blessing our declaration of faith, by declaring it in the following way:

*The Lord blesses me and protects me.*
*His face shines upon me and He is gracious to me.*
*He shows me favor and gives me peace.*

This is our reality as believers. Because of the redemptive work of Christ, we are now living in the favor and blessings of God. He constantly smiles upon us and we are living in the year of the favor of the Lord (Luke 4:17-19). We have divine protection and we are surrounded by the peace of God. We are the blessed and favored bride of Christ, and He will not rest until we walk in all the blessings that He purchased for us through the cross.

## Activations

- Set aside 20-30 minutes for prayer. Ask the Holy Spirit to give deeper insight on the fact that Jesus has dissolved every curse and that the Father has blessed you with all spiritual blessings in Christ. How does that change your perspective on who you are in Christ? Write down what He reveals to you.

- Read the list from this chapter that lists the curses that has been broken once again. Are there one or more of these curses that still operate in your life? Take some time to pray and break these curses. Ask the Holy Spirit if there are steps you can take to find greater freedom in these areas.

- Read the list of blessings from Deuteronomy 28 again. Which one of these blessings do you want to see greater manifestations of in your life? Take time to declare and pray these blessings over your life. Ask the Holy Spirit if there are steps you can take to partner with the blessings. You can do this boldly, knowing that the Father wants a full manifestation of every blessing in your life.

- Read the high priestly blessing again. Take time to pray through this blessing. Declare and pray it regularly over your life, family, children and descendants in prayer. This blessing is the Father's will for you and your family!

# CHAPTER 16: JESUS IS OUR FRIEND

One of the greatest blessings of the New Covenant is that Jesus calls us His friends. In fact, He wants to be our best friend, which is an incredible honor: *"Henceforth I call you not servants; for the servant knoweth not what his lord doeth: but I have called you friends; for all things that I have heard of my Father I have made known unto you"* (John 15:15). Before, when I was reading this passage, I got stuck on the part where Jesus said that we are His friends if we obey His commandments (John 15:14). I thought that this meant to walk in complete obedience and I knew that I couldn't do that. To me that indicated that I was not a real friend of Jesus. But that is not what Jesus meant. He tells us earlier in the gospel of John what it means to obey His commands: *"Then said they unto him, what shall we do, that we might work the works of God? Jesus answered and said unto them, This is the work of God, that ye believe on him whom he hath sent"* (John 6:28-29). We do what Jesus commands by believing in Him and by trusting in His finished work. This is good news because it means that we who believe in Him are His best friends!

## Abraham Was God's Friend

Abraham walked in deep friendship with God long before the New Covenant was established. He is called God's friend several times in the Scriptures. *"And the scripture was fulfilled which saith, Abraham believed God, and it was imputed unto him for righteousness: and he was called the Friend of God"* (Jam. 2:23). As the father of faith, Abraham walked in such a deep intimacy with God that he had access to New Covenant blessings long before they had become operational. God's friendship with Abraham affected how He dealt with Israel even centuries after Abraham had died.

*But you, Israel, My servant, Jacob whom I have chosen, descendant of Abraham My friend, you whom I have taken from the ends of the earth And called from its remotest parts, and said to you, 'You are My servant, I have chosen you and have not rejected you (Isa. 41:8-9 NASB see also 2 Chron. 20:7).*

When we respond to the heavenly invitation to friendship with Jesus, it will impact the world more than we think. Learning to live in intimate friendship with Jesus Christ releases the presence and power of God to impact people for the gospel in a powerful way. Because friendship with Jesus doesn't look like "practical Christianity", we sometimes don't realize how much a friend of Jesus can impact this world. But when studying the friends of God within the Scriptures, we'll find some occasions when their relationship with God changed everything. Abraham is one of the best examples of this.

### God Shares His Heart with Abraham

On day when Abraham was relaxing under the shade of an oak in the heat of the day, he received some very special visitors.

*Now the Lord appeared to Abraham by the oaks of Mamre, while he was sitting at the tent door in the heat of the day. When he raised his eyes and looked, behold, three men were standing opposite him; and when he saw them, he ran from the tent door to meet them and bowed down to the ground (Gen. 18:1-2 NASB).*

Abraham received a personal visit from the Lord, which turned out to be one of these occasions when Jesus showed up in His pre-incarnate form. Jesus explains to some religious leaders that Abraham saw the day of Jesus and rejoiced:

*Your father Abraham rejoiced to see my day: and he saw it, and was glad. Then said the Jews unto him, Thou art not yet fifty years old, and hast thou seen Abraham? Jesus said unto them, Verily, verily, I say unto you, Before Abraham was, I am (John 8:56-58).*

Abraham carried a deep revelation of Jesus, which is always the starting point when it comes to knowing Him in deeper ways. Everything in our relationship with God starts with a revelation of His heart. This visit from the Lord was important because it was during this occasion Abraham received a promise that Isaac was to be born within a year. Finally, Abraham and Sarah were going to receive their child of promise (Gen. 18:9-15).

After they had eaten, the Lord and His companions arose to go to Sodom. Abraham was joining them for a while to say goodbye and send them off. This is when the Lord gives us a hint of how much He values true friendship. *"The Lord said, "Shall I hide from Abraham what I am about to do, since Abraham will certainly become a great and mighty nation, and in him all the nations of the earth will be blessed?" (Gen. 18:17-18 NASB).* The Lord considered Abraham such a good friend that He could not hide His plans from him. That Jesus is sharing the secrets of His heart with us, is the essence of friendship with God. Jesus was expressing this reality when He said that He shares everything that He hears from His Father with us. For Jesus, this is a sign of true friendship. But friendship with the Lord can go even deeper than that. Abraham was able to influence the outcome of God's plan by sharing his heart with the Lord in prayer.

### The Lord Listens to Abraham

*"And the Lord said, "The outcry of Sodom and Gomorrah is indeed great, and their sin is exceedingly grave. I will go down now and see whether they have done entirely as the outcry, which has come to Me*

*indicates; and if not, I will know" (Gen. 18:20-21 NASB).* As the Lord shares His plans to execute the judgement against Sodom and Gomorrah, Abraham responds by asking the Lord if He is going to destroy the righteous with the wicked. He continues by asking the Lord to spare the cities if there are still fifty righteous people in Sodom. The Lord agrees to spare these cities if He finds fifty righteous people within it. Abraham does not stop there. He keeps on asking the Lord to spare the cities if He can find forty-five, then forty and thirty. The Lord grants Abraham this request as well. Abraham continues asking God to spare Sodom if twenty righteous people can be found there. Abraham keeps pressing on all the way to ten righteous people. The Lord listens to Abraham and agrees to spare the city if there are ten righteous people living in it (Gen. 18:22-33). The heart of the Lord is deeply moved by Abraham's prayer. Sadly, it turned out that there were not even ten righteous people living in Sodom and Gomorrah, so these cities were destroyed by a rain of fire and brimstone (Gen. 19:23-29). These cities have now become a symbol of the fate of the wicked, who will perish in the lake of fire. But what would have happened if Abraham had kept on stretching his request for Sodom to be spared? Maybe the city could have been saved.

We are friends of Jesus and our prayer influences His heart. This means that through prayer we can have a tremendous impact on history, but it speaks about the humility of the Lord as well. Jesus is prepared to listen to us as we share the requests of our heart with Him, and through prayer we partner with Him in extending the Kingdom of God. Jesus has left a part of the future open to our choices, where we will be part of deciding the outcome. This is how much Jesus trusts His friends.

## Moses Spoke to the Lord Face to Face

Another friend of God, who lived during Old Testament times but still had encounters with Jesus, was Moses. His revelation of Jesus provided grace and strength to persevere as the leader of the people of God (Hebr. 11:23-27). We looked at this in an earlier chapter, but the relationship of Moses and the Lord reveals even clearer how much friendship with God touches His heart. *"So the Lord used to speak to Moses face to face, just as a man speaks to his friend. When Moses returned to the camp, his servant Joshua, the son of Nun, a young man, would not depart from the tent" (Exod. 33:11 NASB).* Moses was able to speak with the Lord as a friend, which shows us that friendship with God opened the door for Moses to walk in New Covenant realities during Old Testament times.

Moses spoke with the Lord face to face and this friendship was so important to the Lord that it is mentioned in the Word of God (Deut. 34:10). In fact, God had invited all the people of Israel to have a face-to-face relationship with Him, but they were afraid and rejected that invitation. Instead, they requested of Moses to be a mediator between them and God (Deut. 5:1-4). Moses acted as a mediator between the Lord and His people for the rest of his life. Let's look at one particularly dramatic event where Moses' friendship with God saved the people of Israel from perishing.

## God Listens to Moses and Changes His Mind

Moses had gone up to mount Sinai to meet with God. This was the occasion when he received the tablets of stone with the ten commandments. Moses stayed upon the mountain for forty days (Exod. 24:18). The people of Israel got impatient and decided to take matters into their own hands. So, they made a golden calf which they called their God and started to worship it. They even arranged a feast in honor of the calf. This was not the last time that the people of God tried to remake Him into their own image. This behavior made God so upset that He told Moses that He wanted to destroy the people: *"Then the Lord said, "I have seen how stubborn and rebellious these people are. Now leave me alone so my fierce anger can blaze against them, and I will destroy them. Then I will make you, Moses, into a great nation." (Exod. 32:9-10 NLT)*. God was very clear with His intentions. He wanted to destroy the people and start over again with Moses and his offspring.

Moses started to intercede and plead with God. He made the case that if God would kill the people, the other nations and Egypt in particular, could accuse God of having evil intentions, and that He had saved the people of Israel just to kill them Himself (Exod. 32:11-12). Moses then asks God: *"Turn away from your fierce anger. Change your mind about this terrible disaster you have threatened against your people" (Exod. 32:12 NLT)*. He basically told God that this was a bad idea and that God needed to change His mind. He reminded God of His covenant with their forefathers:

*Remember Abraham, Isaac, and Israel, Your servants to whom You swore by Yourself, and said to them, 'I will multiply your descendants as the stars of the heavens, and all this land of which I have spoken I will give to your descendants, and they shall inherit it forever (Exod. 32:13 NASB).*

This was a bold prayer, but God's response is even more mind-blowing: *"So the Lord changed his mind about the terrible disaster he had threatened to bring on his people" (Exod. 32:14 NLT)*. The Lord listened to Moses and changed His mind.

Many different explanations have been offered concerning how this was possible. There is no need to get into these speculations here. The point is that Moses and God were friends, which gave Moses the ability to influence God. He valued the friendship that

He shared with Moses so much, that He even allowed Moses to influence His plans. This is the power of friendship with Jesus.

## Prophets Are Friends of God

So far, we have discovered that friendship with God means that He shares the secrets of His heart with us and that a friend of God can influence history. This is the essence of the prophetic as well. The prophets are friends of God. *"Surely the Lord GOD will do nothing, but he revealeth his secret unto his servants the prophets. The lion hath roared, who will not fear? the Lord GOD hath spoken, who can but prophesy" (Amos 3:7-8)?* Anyone who wants to grow in the prophetic, needs to start by cultivating a deeper friendship with Jesus. That will give access to the heart of God and it is the pathway to walk in the Spirit of revelation. No one illustrates this truth better than John, the apostle. He was one the closest friends of Jesus.

## John — the Disciple Whom Jesus Loved

The life and ministry of John is an invitation to deeper intimacy with Jesus. The following verse pretty much sums up who John is: *"Now there was leaning on Jesus' bosom one of his disciples, whom Jesus loved" (John 13:23).* John lived with a constant posture of leaning on Jesus. This passage is a quote from the gospel of John, which obviously was written by the apostle himself. He referred to himself as the disciple "whom Jesus loved" because he found his identity in being loved by Jesus. This is not the only place where John calls himself that. In fact, John refers to himself as the beloved disciple five different times (John 13:23, 19:26, 20:2, 21:7, 20). John could have chosen to speak of himself in many ways. He was both an apostle and a prophet. He was an author and a honored elder, but these things were not where John placed his identity. His identity was firmly rooted in him being the disciple whom Jesus loved.

### Friendship with Jesus Is the Place of Revelation

Our place of revelation is found in leaning on Jesus, asking Him questions, just like John did. We will now read from John chapter 13 again, but this time from The Passion Translation:

*The disciple that Jesus dearly loved was at the right of him at the table and was leaning his head on Jesus. Peter gestured to this disciple to ask Jesus who it was he was referring to. Then the dearly loved disciple leaned into Jesus' chest and whispered, 'Master, who is it?' (John 13:23-25 TPT).*

As we are leaning on Jesus and come to Him with our questions, we will always find revelation. This is the place where mysteries are revealed and destinies are unlocked. John gained the trust of Jesus because his heart was set on deeper intimacy with Him. When we abide in His love, we become trustworthy stewards of revelation. Jesus can trust His friends with the things that really matter to Him. For this reason, Jesus asked John to take care of His mother as He returned to the right hand of the Father in heaven.

*When Jesus therefore saw His mother, and the disciple whom He loved standing by, He said to His mother, "Woman, behold your son!" Then He said to the disciple, "Behold your mother!" And from that hour that disciple took her to his own home (John 19:26-27 NKJV).*

Developing friendship with Jesus is the only true way to become a trustworthy steward with a pure heart. It is good idea to have friends, mentors and to be part of a community of believers where we can live in transparency and develop accountability.

That can certainly help us to stay on track with God and to live a life of purity. I have benefitted immensely from these myself. But the history of the church is full of leaders who had all this, but still fell into sin and sometimes even lost their faith. Only intimacy with Jesus Himself will protect our hearts. Only by abiding in His presence can we be conformed into His image.

## John the Revelator

John was the disciple whom Jesus loved, but he was also a seer prophet who saw into the depths of God's heart, where mysteries were revealed to him. This culminated as John received the Book of Revelation through a vision. All of John's writings are full of revelations on the love of Christ and the heart of the Father. But the Book of Revelation is a deep vision of the plans of the Father, revealing Jesus and His eternal victory. Within this book, we get profound insight into the New Covenant and the bride of Christ. This beautiful vision reveals Jesus as the Lion and Lamb of God (Rev. 5:5-6). The book of Revelation is the most prophetic book in the Bible, and it is significant that this revelation was entrusted to the disciple whom Jesus loved. Jesus cannot hide his plans from His friends.

## We are the Disciples Whom Jesus Loves

We are the disciples whom Jesus loves and we have a face-to-face friendship with Him. Jesus wants to reveal the secrets of His heart to us and He wants us to be partners with Him through our prayers. To be His friends means that we are living a lifestyle of revelation. We carry the anointing of intimacy that spreads the sweet fragrance of the presence of Jesus wherever we go. There is no friend like Jesus, our Bridegroom. He is the funniest, most faithful, loving, and interesting friend in the whole universe!

# Activations

- Set aside 20-30 minutes for prayer. Ask the Holy Spirit for deeper insight into the meaning of friendship with Jesus. How does your perspective of life as a believer change when you view it as life of friendship with Jesus? Write down what He reveals to you.

- Within this chapter, we have looked at John, Moses, and Abraham as examples of people who were close friends with God. Find two or three good examples of people who were friends of God. Study their lives and ask the Holy Spirit to teach you about being a friend of Jesus by using their lives.

- Take time in prayer with Jesus and ask Him to deepen your friendship. Ask Jesus to be your best friend and spend some quality time with Him, speaking to Him face to face like a friend.

- The stories of Abraham, Moses and John, inspire us to cultivate a deeper friendship with Jesus. Ask Jesus to use your life as an inspiration for other people to cultivate a deeper friendship with Jesus. Ask Him for the grace of imparting friendship with Jesus to the body of Christ.

# CHAPTER 17: JESUS - OUR BRIDEGROOM AND KING

Jesus is our Bridegroom, but He is our Lord and King as well. He is the only true head of His body. Jesus alone can provide the leadership and grace necessary for us to grow into a mature bride that moves in kingly authority. He possesses all the wisdom and power necessary to make that happen, and He is working toward that end right now. Daniel received an interesting and powerful vision, which reveals Jesus as ruler and king over the nations:

*I kept looking in the night visions, and behold, with the clouds of heaven one like a son of man was coming, and He came up to the Ancient of Days and was presented before Him. "And to Him was given dominion, honor, and a kingdom, so that all the peoples, nations, and populations of all languages might serve Him. His dominion is an everlasting dominion which will not pass away; and His kingdom is one which will not be destroyed (Dan 7:13-14 NASB).*

This prophecy speaks of the ascension of Jesus, which took place after He had been raised from the dead and ascended to the right hand of the Father. As Jesus was enthroned in the heavens, all authority in heaven and earth was given to Him (Matt. 28:18). Jesus is right now seated in the heavenlies, where He will reign as King, until the Kingdom of God has been extended all over the earth. *"And the seventh angel sounded; and there were great voices in heaven, saying, the kingdoms of this world are become the kingdoms of our Lord, and of his Christ; and he shall reign for ever and ever."* (Rev. 11:15).

**My Experience of Knowing Jesus as The Victorious King**

Knowing Jesus as the victorious King was a major upgrade for my relationship with God. When I was working as a pastor some years ago, I realized that many of the members in the church where I served, had a dark and defeatist view of the future. Other members didn't want to mention this subject at all. I discovered that the reason for this was that they had heard a lot of fear-based teaching on the end-times. But fear never comes from God, so I realized that we needed a better understanding on this subject in our church. As I studied what the Scriptures has to say about our future, I found that it holds to a very optimistic and victorious view of our future with Jesus. The biblical view can basically be summed in the following way: *Jesus reigns and the Kingdom of God will break through into all spheres of society until it is extended all over the world.* This revelation has led me to reject every view of our future that undermines this reality. Any view of the end-times that that empowers the devil, or that does not envision how the Kingdom of God will continue to grow, is incompatible with a Kingdom-centered view of the future. Jesus is presently ruling as King and we're reigning in life together with Him (Rom. 5:17).

**Jesus Reigns until Every Enemy Is Put under His Feet**

King David was a man who had deep insight into the authority of God. As a prophet, David carried a powerful revelation of the coming Messiah and the New Covenant. He wrote a prophetic Psalm that pointed to the coming reign of Jesus Christ, our King:

*The Lord says to my Lord: "Sit at My right hand Until I make Your enemies a footstool for Your feet." The Lord will stretch out Your strong scepter from Zion, saying, "Rule in the midst of Your enemies." Your people will volunteer freely on the day of Your power (Ps. 110:1-3 NASB).*

The events within this Psalm took place right after the death and resurrection of Christ. The Lord then ascended and sat down at the right hand of the Father to reign. Jesus is now reigning and He is making sure that the gospel will be proclaimed all over the world. As a result of that, every enemy of Christ will be placed under His feet, one after another. A Jesus-centered view of our future with God must reveal how Jesus is transforming the world by extending the Kingdom. All synoptic gospels each quote these verses from Psalm 110 about the present reign of Jesus:

*"What do you think about the Christ? Whose son is He?" They said to Him, "The son of David." He said to them, "Then how does David in the Spirit call Him 'Lord,' saying, 'The Lord said to my Lord, Sit at My right hand, Until I put Your enemies under Your feet'?" (Matt. 22:42-44 NASB see also Mark 12:35-37, Luke 20:41-44).*

Peter quoted the same passage while he preached on the day of Pentecost, as did the author of Hebrews (Acts 2:34-35, Hebr. 1:13, 10:12-13). By noticing that so many of the biblical authors quoted this psalm, we find how important it is to the God that we know that Jesus is King and that we have a victorious future with Him.

### Encouraged by a Vision of Our Victorious Future

As the body of Christ gets a revelation of Jesus as the ruling King who has given us a victorious future, we will be even more empowered to partner with His vision of the Kingdom of God transforming this world. In fact, this vision will move us to the point where we are ready to give up everything just to see the purposes of God manifesting in this world. We will *volunteer freely in the day of Your power"*. The period described as "the day of His power" refers to the New Covenant. We are living in that day now and God is raising up a people who willingly joins our King in extending His Kingdom. When Paul writes his letter to the Corinthians explaining the resurrection of the dead and the end of the ages, he refers to this prophetic Psalm in the following way: *"For Christ must reign [as King] until He has put all His enemies under His feet. The last enemy to be abolished and put to an end is death. For He (the Father) has put all things in subjection under His (Christ's) feet"* (1 Cor. 15:25-27 AMP).

Jesus will reign until the Kingdom of God has been established in every nation, tribe and people group. Then He will return for His bride. At the time of His return, the bride will reign in kingly authority, being busy placing all enemies under the feet of Jesus. This will not happen through political means or social activism. The Kingdom of God does not align itself with either the political right or the political left. This will happen through the preaching of the gospel by a bride who has been captivated by Jesus Christ. After the return of Christ, when all His enemies are defeated, He will hand his Kingdom over to the Father. *"When all things are subjected to Him, then the Son Himself will also be subjected to the One who subjected all things to Him, so that God may be all in all"* (1 Cor 15:28 NASB).

## Jesus Is the King of Kings

Jesus is the called the King of kings, and He is leading an army of chosen and faithful followers into a spiritual war in which He is victorious. *"These shall make war with the Lamb, and the Lamb shall overcome them: for he is Lord of lords, and King of kings: and they that are with him are called, and chosen, and faithful"* (Rev. 17:14 see also 1 Tim. 6:15-16). Jesus is ruler of the nations and He has authority over the kings of the earth (Rev. 1:5, 19:15-16). That makes Jesus King of kings, but there is an important implication in that name for us as well. Since we are His royal priesthood, who are going to rule the nations with Jesus, we are his kings in this world (Rev.

2:26-27). He is our King, which makes Him King of kings within the church as well, as among the nations.

We are a royal priesthood, commissioned by Jesus to extend the Kingdom of God all over the world. *"For if by one man's offence death reigned by one; much more they which receive abundance of grace and of the gift of righteousness shall reign in life by one, Jesus Christ" (Rom. 5:17).* The way Jesus releases His kingly authority on the earth today is through His body. We have been made His kings and ambassadors in this world. We are now in a process of being conformed into His image. An important aspect of that process is that we are training for reigning, meaning that we are being prepared to reign with Jesus. He is Lord right now, and we have been seated with Him in heavenly places (Eph. 2:6). We reign in life together with Jesus.

## Jesus Rules in Sacrificial Love

When reading the book of Revelation, it is important to realize that it is a prophetic book, written to reveal the victory of Jesus Christ. It is not mainly a book pointing to future events. Instead, it is written in a prophetic language to unveil Jesus and the New Covenant. Jesus is revealed as the King of kings within this book. Since Jesus has all authority, He can do whatever He wants. Yet, He has chosen to rule in grace and humility. Jesus received the kingdom because He humbled Himself by going to the cross. Jesus gave His life to redeem us and make us His bride. Because He delivered us from sin through His blood, He could make us into a kingdom of priests to the Father: *"…and from Jesus Christ, the faithful witness, the firstborn of the dead, and the ruler of the kings of the earth. To Him who loves us and released us from our sins by His blood— and He made us into a kingdom, priests to His God and Father—to Him be the glory and the dominion forever and ever. Amen" (Rev. 1:5-6 NASB).*

Jesus always uses His kingly authority in humility and sacrificial love. As we're growing in spiritual authority, we must remember the way of the Lamb of God, which is meekness and divine love.

### The King of Kings in the Book of Revelation

John received the Book of Revelation through a prophetic vision, and within this vision he received a powerful revelation of Jesus as the King of Kings. His appearance within this vision is indeed awe inspiring:

*And I saw heaven opened, and behold, a white horse, and He who sat on it is called Faithful and True, and in righteousness He judges and wages war. His eyes are a flame of fire, and on His head are many crowns; and He has a name written on Him which no one knows except Himself. He is clothed with a robe dipped in blood, and His name is called The Word of God. And the armies which are in heaven, clothed in fine linen, white and clean, were following Him on white horses. From His mouth comes a sharp sword, so that with it He may strike down the nations, and He will rule them with a rod of iron; and He treads the wine press of the fierce wrath of God, the Almighty. And on His robe and on His thigh He has a name written: "KING OF KINGS, AND Lord OF LORDS" (Rev. 19:11-16 NASB).*

A misreading of this passage has given birth to a lot of wrong ideas about Jesus. For example, some people have thought that this is a description of Jesus appearing full of wrath, coming to get even with humanity. There will be a judgement day where Jesus will judge the world, but His heart is not full of vengeance. Jesus loves mercy and He is quick to forgive (Jonah 4:2, Micah 6:8). This passage is speaking about the spiritual battle where Jesus leads His people in victory, executing judgement against Satan and the realm of darkness to bring salvation to the world. This vision reveals who Jesus is, and by looking at some of the symbolic language within it, we can find several powerful truths about our wonderful Bridegroom and King. Here are some of these truths:

- *Jesus Sits on a White Horse.* The white horse is a symbol of the gospel going forth in victory. We saw earlier in this book how Jesus was riding on this horse alone as the gospel went forth into the world (Rev. 6:1-2). In this vision, Jesus is leading an army consisting of the people who have been won by the preaching of the gospel. We know that Jesus has already overcome every enemy through the cross, but right now these enemies are being placed under His feet, as He is leading us forth to occupy spiritual territory and enforce His victory (2 Cor. 2:14-15).

- *Jesus is Faithful and True.* Jesus is full of grace and truth and He is the faithful witness (John 1:14, Rev. 1:5). The words of Jesus are true and fully reliable. He is the Word of God and whatever He speaks forth will always come to pass. Since Jesus is faithful and true, there is no deception in Him. His judgements are executed in righteousness. We can be confident that Jesus will always keep His promises. *"For all the promises of God in Him are Yes, and in Him Amen, to the glory of God through us"* (2 Cor. 1:20 NKJV).

- *His eyes are like a flame of fire.* We have mentioned several times in this book that the eyes of Jesus are a flame of fire, burning with love for His bride (Song. 8:6). Jesus has a burning passion for us, which can be seen in His eyes (Rev. 1:14, 2:18). Jesus' gaze burns with a holy love as He is looking at His bride.

- *On His head are many crowns.* Jesus wears many crowns because He has the authority over all powers and principalities. Jesus reigns and He possesses all authority in heaven and on earth (Matt. 28:18). Jesus reigns in the heavens right now and every crown of authority are rightfully His because He has won an eternal victory through the cross (Rev. 12:10).

- *He is clothed with a robe dipped in blood.* His robe is dipped in blood, but it is not dipped in the blood of His enemies. The robe of Jesus Christ is dipped in the blood of the Lamb, which is His own blood that was shed for our sake. A revelation of the blood of Jesus Christ is the foundation for spiritual authority in the Kingdom of God. It is His blood that is our guarantee for victory in every battle (Rev. 12:11).

- *His name is called The Word of God.* Jesus is the final Word of God and the fulfillment of both the law and the prophets (Matt. 5:17-18). Everything that the Father ever wanted to communicate about Himself, has now been fully revealed in Jesus Christ. Jesus is the complete revelation of the Father and He is the Word of God (Hebr. 1:1-2).

- *From His mouth comes a sharp sword, so that with it He may strike down the nations.* Jesus wages a spiritual war for the salvation of man. This is a war against the principalities and powers that want to ruin humanity. The sharp sword that is coming out of the mouth of Jesus is the gospel (Hebr. 4:12-13). The nations will be struck open by the Word of God, as we make disciples of all nations by the preaching of the gospel (Matt. 28:18-20). All resistance to the gospel of Jesus Christ will fall, and the nations will be transformed into the Kingdom of our God. Jesus will have a bride, consisting of people from nations and tribes in the world (Rev. 7:9).

- *He will rule them with a rod of iron.* This rod of iron is the shepherd's rod (Ps. 23:4). The iron speaks of His firmness in leading the nations according to His purposes, but Jesus is the good shepherd. He reigns in gentleness and humility (John 10:11). He operates as the shepherd of the nations by leading them home to the Father. Jesus is making sure that His will for every nation is coming to pass, but He is not doing it alone. Jesus rules the nations together with His bride (Rev. 2:26-27).

- *He treads the wine press of the fierce wrath of God, the Almighty.* The fierce wrath of God is not directed at us, but against Satan and the realm of darkness. Satan with all his principalities and powers, as well as sin and death, suffers the wrath of God. His wrath is revealed as the power of Jesus Christ sets people free by destroying the works of Satan (1 John 3:8). Jesus won a complete victory over the devil at the cross and stripped him of all authority. But now, we are enforcing His victory by preaching the gospel and destroying the works of darkness.

- *On His robe and on His thigh He has a name written: "KING OF KINGS, AND LORD OF LORDS".* This name does not need much explanation. Jesus is King over all other kings, and He is the rightful Lord over every lord (Rev. 5:11-12). Jesus now has all authority, which means that no other ruler has any real power.

All power and authority belong to Jesus Christ and He will reign forever and ever.

Jesus is the King of kings, but He rules and reigns in sacrificial love and humility. He is the only one who can handle to have all authority, while at the same time rule with humility. Jesus is an amazing king! Within this vision, there was an army following Jesus into the battle. That army is the bride of Christ, who has been trained and equipped by Jesus Himself.

## Trained by the King

This is how the warrior-bride of Christ looks in the Spirit. *"He wore a robe dipped in blood, and his title is called the Word of God. Following him on white horses were the armies of heaven, wearing white fine linen, pure and bright" (Rev. 19:13-14 TPT).* This army consists of us who have been seated in heavenly places with Jesus Christ. We are clothed in fine linen, that is white and clean, which point to our righteousness and perfection in Christ (Rev. 19:8). We are the warrior-bride who has answered His call to join the battle voluntarily and freely. *"Your people will offer themselves willingly [to participate in Your battle] in the day of Your power; In the splendor of holiness, from the womb of the dawn, your young men are to You as the dew" (Ps. 110:3 AMP).*

## King David and His Mighty Men

David is an important Old Testament type of Christ, especially when it comes to knowing Jesus as the King of kings. There is a part of David's story that paints a very good picture of how Jesus is raising up His bride. When David was hiding from king Saul, he was visited by a group of men, who needed leadership and guidance. These men did not look very impressive. In fact, they were very frustrated and discontent with life. They found David in the cave of Adullam: *"Then everyone who was in distress, and everyone who was in debt, and everyone who was discontented gathered to him; and he became captain over them. Now there were about four hundred men with him"* (1 Sam 22:1-2 NASB). This group of people, who joined David in the wilderness were stuck in distress and debt, but David gave them hope of change. He even became their captain and he trained them in the ways of God.

This discontented group saw kingly authority and a prophetic destiny within David's life. David changed them from a group of grumbling and frustrated men his into mighty warriors. They became David's fiercest warriors and most loyal supporters. The things that they accomplished in battle were so incredible that the only explanation was that they were empowered by God (see 2 Sam. 23:8-39, 1 Chron. 11:10-47). We are the mighty warrior-bride of Jesus Christ, but it is rare to find a believer or a church whose life reflects this. Right now, Jesus is calling us to embrace our bridal identity. As we are responding to that call, we will be transformed into mighty men and women of God, whom Jesus will use to do extraordinary exploits to extend His Kingdom.

### Jesus Sits on the Throne of David

David is a type of Jesus as our King, embodying what true spiritual authority and leadership is supposed to look like. The Bible even declares that Jesus rules from the throne of David. David's leadership was built on worship and intimacy with God. The prophet Isaiah reveals how Jesus now rules from the throne of David, continually increasing His government of peace:

*For a Child will be born to us, a Son will be given to us; and the government will rest on His shoulders; and His name will be called Wonderful Counselor, Mighty God, Eternal Father, Prince of Peace. There will be no end to the increase of His government or of peace on*

Just like the mighty men were transformed because they saw a kingly authority in David, so our journey starts by us receiving a revelation of Jesus. As we behold the glory of Jesus, we will find new hope. When we submit to Jesus as our King and leader, we will be transformed into mighty and joyful children of God. These mighty men did powerful exploits to extend and establish the kingdom of Israel. As we submit to Jesus, we will do mighty exploits that will extend and establish the Kingdom of God all over the world. Jesus will reign until every enemy has been put under His feet and the Kingdom of our God has transformed the world. Jesus is the King of kings forever!

## Activations

- Set aside 20-30 minutes for prayer. Ask the Holy Spirit to reveal Jesus as the King of kings in a deeper way. Ask Him to provide more insight on the kingly authority of Jesus and how you can reign with Him in life right now. Write down the insights He gives to you.

- Read the passage from the book of Revelation, in which Jesus is revealed as the King of kings (Rev. 19:11-16). Then read the list I made based on this passage. Ask the Holy Spirit to highlight some of the points on that list. Invite Him to reveal more of Jesus through these points.

- How does adapting a victorious view of the future with Jesus change your perspective? Invite the Father to share His perspectives on the future with you. Ask the Holy Spirit to fill your heart with a new and victorious vision for the future. Write down this vision and use it in prayer for your life and calling.

- Jesus is your Lord and King. Invite Him to reveal more of His lordship to you. Then ask Him to reveal how you can submit to Him in a deeper way. Write down the steps He will show you and act on them.

# CHAPTER 18: JESUS IS OUR HIGH PRIEST

Jesus is our King, but He is our High Priest as well. He has made us into a royal priesthood, meaning that we are now His kings and priests. Jesus did this by delivering us from our sins through His blood (Rev. 1:5-6). The ministry of Christ as King and Priest goes together. While the book of Revelation majors on Jesus being the King of kings, the letter to the Hebrews makes the high priestly ministry of Christ its main point. *"Now the main point in what has been said is this: we have such a high priest, who has taken His seat at the right hand of the throne of the Majesty in the heavens, a minister in the sanctuary and in the true tabernacle, which the Lord set up, not man" (Hebr. 8:1-2 NASB).* Jesus could take His seat because His work was finished. He had offered one sacrifice for sins for all time and by doing so, Jesus carried away the sins of the world (John 1:29).

Not only did Jesus solve the problem of sin and guilt through the cross, but He established a new and better covenant as well. *"But now hath he obtained a more excellent ministry, by how much also he is the mediator of a better covenant, which was established upon better promises" (Hebr. 8:6).* The reason that Jesus was able to do this is because he was not a priest according to the law and the Levitical order. The law and its priesthood could never solve the problem of sin, which the repeated sacrifices of atonement for the sins of Israel attested to (Hebr. 10:1-4). But Jesus dealt with the problem of sin once and for all through the cross. He defeated sin in such a complete way that no other sacrifice will ever be needed. We are both forgiven and perfected through the one sacrifice of Jesus Christ (Hebr. 10:10-18). This was all made possible because Jesus was a priest according to the order of Melchizedek (Hebr. 6:19-20).

# According to the Order of Melchizedek

The order of Melchizedek brings us back to Psalm 110, which we studied in the previous chapter, particularly the first three verses of this psalm. We know that this is a messianic Psalm, and it speaks about Jesus being a priest in the order of Melchizedek. *"The Lord has sworn and will not change his mind: "You are a priest forever, in the order of Melchizedek" (Ps.110:4 NIV).* The Lord gave an oath, promising that Jesus will be a priest forever. Since His priesthood cannot be changed, the New Covenant will never change either. This is an everlasting covenant, which cannot be dissolved or broken. In the letter to the Hebrews, we'll find the most extensive teaching on the eternal priesthood of Christ and the order of Melchizedek. But before we dive into the book of Hebrews, we need to look at the one passage where Melchizedek shows up in person:

*And Melchizedek the king of Salem brought out bread and wine; now he was a priest of God Most High. And he blessed him and said, "Blessed be Abram of God Most High, Possessor of heaven and earth; And blessed be God Most High, who has handed over your enemies to you." And he gave him a tenth of everything (Gen. 14:18-20 NASB).*

There are several similarities between Jesus and Melchizedek. This mysterious man was a king and a priest of God. His name means *king of righteousness.* Melchizedek was the king of a city called Salem. The name Salem means peace, so Melchizedek was *the king of peace* (Hebr. 7:2). We know nothing of Melchizedek's ancestral line, and there is nothing written when it comes to the circumstances concerning his birth or death. He remains a priest to this day and he has no successor (Hebr. 7:1-3). Melchizedek was not a descendant of Aaron and was therefore not a priest of the Levitical order (Hebr. 7:11-12).

## Jesus Was a Priest of the Order of Melchizedek

Just like Melchizedek, Jesus was not a priest according to the Levitical order. He came from the tribe of Judah, so for Jesus to become priest, there needed to be a change of covenant (Hebr. 7:14). We know that this change happened through the cross, which means that the order of Melchizedek is not based on the bloodline of Aaron. Both Melchizedek and Jesus became priests *"…after the power of an endless life. For he testifieth, Thou art a priest for ever after the order of Melchizedec" (Hebr. 7:16-17).* Only Jesus lived a sinless life, but Melchizedek was a priest whose days had neither beginning nor end. This is what an endless life refers to here. Only Jesus is our perfect, sinless and spotless lamb who fulfilled the law and the prophets completely (Matt. 5:17-18). Therefore, He can be our priest and mediator. The priesthood of Jesus was not only based on His perfect life, but the Father gave Jesus His oath that Jesus would be a priest forever: *"The Lord has sworn and will not change His mind, 'You are a priest forever'; by the same extent Jesus also has become the guarantee of a better covenant"* *(Hebr. 7:21-22 NASB).*

## Melchizedek Is a Type of Christ

Most of us have probably already figured out that Melchizedek is a picture of Jesus Christ. The obvious similarities they share has led many people to believe that Melchizedek was another one of Jesus' appearances in pre-incarnate form. There are quite many such appearances to be found within the Old Testament, which is to be expected, since it was written as a witness of Jesus Christ. Whether we believe that Melchizedek is Jesus appearing in the Old Testament or not, we can all agree that Melchizedek is one of the most obvious pictures of Jesus Christ within the Old Testament. This is how Melchizedek is a type of Christ:

- *He is a priest, a king, and a prophet (Hebr. 7:1).*
- *He is the king of righteousness and the king of peace (Hebr. 7:2).*
- *He blessed God's chosen one and celebrated his victory with a meal, serving bread and wine (Gen. 14:18).*
- *He is without beginning of days or end of life (Hebr. 7:3).*
- *He remains a priest forever (Hebr.7:3).*
- *He is not a descendant of Levi but became a priest based on an indestructible life (Hebr. 7:6, 16-17).*
- *He is greater than Abraham (Hebr. 7:6-7).*

Melchizedek is a perfect type of the life and priestly ministry of Jesus Christ, our High Priest and King. Melchizedek was much more than an ordinary man. He revealed Jesus in a powerful way and his life still blesses us, even to this day. Even though we do not find it specifically mentioned within the Bible, this makes Melchizedek a prophet as well.

## A Perfect High Priest

That Jesus is a priest forever has important consequences that are extremely good news for us. *"But He, because He continues forever, has an unchangeable priesthood. Therefore He is also able to save to the uttermost those who come to God through Him, since He always lives to make intercession for them"* (Hebr. 7:24-25 NKJV). This means that our salvation through Jesus Christ will last forever. He lives to intercede for us, which shows us that we are always in His heart and on His mind. That gives us an insight into how much Jesus loves and cares about us. He does not want an eternity in heaven without us. Jesus knew that none of us could reach Him on our own, so He gave His life for us. As Jesus ascended to heaven, He brought us with Him and seated us with Him at the right hand of the Father. We are now united with Jesus forever.

*For it was fitting for us to have such a high priest, holy, innocent, undefiled, separated from sinners, and exalted above the heavens; who has no daily need, like those high priests, to offer up sacrifices, first for His own sins and then for the sins of the people, because He did this once for all time when He offered up Himself (Hebr. 7:26-27 NASB).*

The one who is holy and separated from sinners, who is exalted above the heavens, offered Himself up to cleanse us from sin and to raise us from the dead and give us eternal life. Jesus used His power and authority to humble Himself and shower us in the mercy and forgiveness of the Father. That is self-giving love in action, which shows us that Jesus is a perfect High Priest. This makes Him the guarantor for a better covenant.

### A Better Covenant

It is important to understand that the eternal priesthood of Christ is our guarantee of a better covenant (Hebr. 7:21-22). It is a better Covenant because it doesn't depend on human performance. In the Old Covenant, people were blessed if they could obey the law, and cursed if they were disobedient to its commandments. In the New Covenant, we cannot be cursed, and we are blessed because of the vicarious obedience of Christ. Jesus is the "Amen" of the Father to all His promises and blessings (2 Cor. 1:20).

Since we are in Christ, we inherit the Kingdom of God because of the redemptive work of Jesus Himself. *"But now He has obtained a more excellent ministry, to the extent that He is also the mediator of a better covenant, which has been enacted on better promises"* (Hebr. 8:6 NASB). The reason that the New Covenant is better is solely because it rests on the finished work of Jesus Christ. He is our guarantee that the New Covenant will remain forever.

## The Problem with the Old Covenant

*"For if that first covenant had been faultless, then should no place have been sought for the second" (Hebr. 8:7).* Jesus found fault with the Old Covenant, but that had nothing to do with the law. The ten commandments are the revealed will of God and the law is holy, just and good (Rom. 7:12). The problem was that the law couldn't make us holy, just and good. Our brokenness and bondage to sin created this problem since we were unable fulfill our part of the Old Covenant (Rom. 8:1-3). Therefore, a new and better covenant was needed. When the New Covenant was established through the cross of Jesus Christ, the Old Covenant became obsolete. The two covenants existed side by side for a period of time, but when the temple was destroyed during the siege of Jerusalem in about AD 70, the Old Covenant fully disappeared. *"When God speaks of "A new covenant," He makes the first one obsolete. And whatever is becoming obsolete (out of use, annulled) and growing old is ready to disappear" (Hebr. 8:13 AMP).*

## The New Covenant

There are two almost identical passages in the book of Hebrews describing the New Covenant. The first one is found in chapter eight, located right between the verses we just read. This is how the New Covenant is described:

*For this is the covenant which I will make with the house of Israel After those days, declares the Lord: I will put My laws into their minds, and write them on their hearts. And I will be their God, and they shall be My people. "And they will not teach, each one his fellow citizen, and each one his brother, saying, 'Know the Lord,' For they will all know Me, From the least to the greatest of them. For I will be merciful toward their wrongdoings, and their sins I will no longer remember (Hebr. 8:10-12 NASB).*

Notice that there is no "You shall" or "if you", presented within the text. The only one who is making promises within the New Covenant is God Himself. He is the only active part here. This is because the Father chose to establish the New Covenant between Himself and Jesus Christ. We have been included in it by being in Christ. The only condition here is God's *"I will"*, describing what the Father promises to be and do for His children through the New Covenant. We have no obligations to fulfill, other than just saying yes and receive the benefits of the finished work of Jesus. These benefits are ours by grace through faith:

- ***I will put My laws into their minds and write them on their hearts.*** In the New Covenant, we are led by the Holy Spirit who writes the will of God upon our hearts (2 Cor. 3:1-6). He writes the law of Jesus Christ into our spiritual DNA, making it easy for us to know and live in the will of God. It is not hard to know God's will, since we have His purposes written within our spirit. The law that Jesus has written on our hearts is not the law of the Old Covenant. The Holy Spirit writes the law of Christ, which is also called the law of the Spirit of Christ within our hearts (Rom. 8:2, Gal. 6:2). The New Covenant is all about a living relationship with Jesus and the Holy Spirit (2 Cor. 3:4-6).

- ***I will be their God, and they shall be My people.*** The Father promises that He will be our God and we find our identity in being His people. Because we belong to Jesus Christ, we are kings and priest who have been given a new royal identity. Our dignity and innocence have been restored and we receive value and identity by being our Father's beloved and favored children. *"But you are God's chosen treasure —priests who are kings, a spiritual "nation" set apart as God's devoted ones. He called you out of darkness* *to experience his marvelous light, and now he claims you as his very own. He did this so that you would broadcast his glorious wonders throughout the world" (1 Pet. 2:9 TPT).*

- ***For they will all know Me, from the least to the greatest of them.*** We have been given a personal relationship with our heavenly Father and we are in union with Jesus Himself. This is how we know His voice (John 10:3-5). We don't need to be a special people to know Jesus. He has chosen us to be His friends. All His people can know Him and whether we are the least or the greatest in the Kingdom of God makes no difference to Him. We have instant access to Jesus all the time. *"I am the good shepherd; I know my own sheep, and they know me, just as my Father knows me and I know the Father. So I sacrifice my life for the sheep" (John 10:14-15 NLT).*

- ***For I will be merciful toward their wrongdoings, and their sins I will no longer remember.*** All our sins - past, present, and future - have already been forgiven and nailed to the cross (Col. 2:13-15). We are not guilty and condemned anymore. We have received such a complete forgiveness that God no longer remember our sins. We are drenched in the love and mercy of Jesus Christ. *"For at one time you were not God's people, but now you are. At one time you knew nothing of God's mercy, because you hadn't received it yet, but now you are drenched with it" (1 Pet. 2:10 TPT)!*

We live in a glorious time right now, where we can enjoy the full benefits of the New Covenant. The Holy Spirit has written the law of Christ on our hearts. We are a royal and priestly bride, who lives in union with Jesus. We know His voice, and we are so totally forgiven that God no longer remembers our sins.

# The Bondage of the Levitical Priesthood

The priests of the Levitical order had to keep on offering the same sacrifices repeatedly, while they were still standing to minister. Since there were no chairs within the Holy of Holies, they could not sit down. The reason for this was that their work never came to an end. *"And every priest standeth daily ministering and offering oftentimes the same sacrifices, which can never take away sins" (Hebr. 10:11).* The Levitical order of ministry could not bring the people of God into true freedom. Rather, it created an obsession with sin and caused them to view their relationship with God through the lenses of condemnation and separation. The sacrifices of the Old Covenant became a painful reminder of the sinful and broken state of God's people. *"But in those sacrifices there is a remembrance again made of sins every year. For it is not possible that the blood of bulls and of goats should take away sins" (Hebr. 10:3-4 NASB).*

## Sanctified and Perfected Through One Sacrifice

Here we find the radical difference between the priest of the old covenant and our High Priest, Jesus Christ: *"But this Man, after He had offered one sacrifice for sins forever, sat down at the right hand of God, from that time waiting till His enemies are made His footstool" (Hebr. 10:12-13 NKJV).* After Jesus had offered one sacrifice for sins forever, He sat down to rest. His work was finished forever. The sacrifice of Jesus eradicated our sins, while at the same time sanctifying and perfecting us as well. The sacrifices of the Old Covenant became a reminder of sin and brokenness. The perfect sacrifice of Jesus Christ reminds us that we have been perfected forever. *"By the which will we are sanctified through the offering of the body of Jesus Christ once for all… For by one offering he hath perfected forever them that are sanctified" (Hebr. 10:10, 14).* Our High Priest took away our sins by one sacrifice for all time, making us a holy and spotless bride, living in union with Him forever. This is the greater glory of the priesthood in the order of Melchizedek.

## No Longer an Offering for Sin

As I mentioned earlier there are two almost identical passages describing the New Covenant in the book of Hebrews. The first one in chapter eight, the second one here in chapter ten: *"This is the covenant that I will make with them After those days, saith the Lord, I will put my laws into their hearts, and in their minds will I write them; and their sins and iniquities will I remember no more. Now where remission of these is, there is no more offering for sin"* (Hebr. 10:16-18). God promises that He doesn't remember our sins anymore. They are no longer an issue in our relationship with the Father. Jesus has dealt with the problem of sin and guilt once and for all through the cross. All our sins have already been forgiven and we no longer need to offer any sacrifices for sins or be tormented by a guilty conscience. We are totally perfected and guilt-free, all because of our amazing High Priest.

## Jesus Is a Merciful High Priest

Throughout this chapter, we have seen the mercy and grace of Jesus, our High Priest. I have always found a lot of comfort in knowing that Jesus knows what it feels like to be human. He can walk with us through our moments of weakness and struggle.

*Therefore, in all things He had to be made like His brethren, that He might be a merciful and faithful High Priest in things pertaining to God, to make propitiation for the sins of the people. For in that He Himself has suffered, being tempted, He is able to aid those who are tempted (Hebr. 2:17-18 NKJV).*

Jesus is faithful and full of mercy. He knows, through personal experience, what it means to deal with human suffering and how tough it is to be human at times. Therefore, He wants to come to our aid when we are tempted. Jesus knows what we feel when we are wrestling with our weakness and He wants to strengthen and encourage us every day. Jesus is very patient with us in our weaknesses, wanting us to come to Him to receive all the mercy and grace we could ever need. Jesus gives more than enough of His grace and mercy to us: *"For we do not have a High Priest who cannot sympathize with our weaknesses, but was in all points tempted as we are, yet without sin. Let us therefore come boldly to the throne of grace, that we may obtain mercy and find grace to help in time of need"* (*Hebr. 4:15-16 NKJV*). Jesus is a great High priest, being full of mercy and grace. He has provided a perfect salvation for us, through which we have been completely forgiven and perfectly sanctified. The gospel is good news.

## The Mount of Transfiguration

We are going to end this chapter by a beautiful illustration on the better promises of the New Covenant, showing how grace can accomplish what the law never could. Most of us are probably familiar with the story of how Jesus changed His appearance on the mount of Transfiguration. Here is what happened:

*Six days later Jesus took Peter and the two brothers, James and John, and led them up a high mountain to be alone. As the men watched, Jesus' appearance was transformed so that his face shone like the sun, and his clothes became as white as light. Suddenly, Moses and Elijah appeared and began talking with Jesus (Matt. 17:1-3 NLT).*

This event is of a highly prophetic significance. On this occasion, Moses and Elijah appeared. Moses represents the law here while Elijah represents the prophets. Then the Father spoke with an audible voice, saying about Jesus: *"This is my dearly loved Son, who brings me great joy. Listen to him" (Matt. 17:5 NLT).* The Father did what He always does, by directing all the attention unto His beloved Son, Jesus Christ. Peter was tempted to place Moses and Elijah on the same level with Jesus. But that cannot be done. Jesus is the fulfillment of the law and the prophets and we cannot mix law and grace without watering down the gospel. So, Moses and Elijah disappeared and the disciples saw only Jesus.

The mount of Transfiguration is located within the promised land. Since Moses had misrepresented God in front of the people, by striking the rock twice, God did not allow him to enter the promised land (Num. 20:12). This was a very painful experience for Moses. But this story still had a happy ending. When Moses and Elijah appeared on the mountain with Jesus, Moses finally stood on the soil of the promised land. He was once again able to speak with Jesus, face to face like a friend. Moses finally made it into the land! What the law could not do, the grace of God did.

If our story hasn't turned out good yet, it means that we have not seen the end of it. Because the Father is writing our story, it will end in a good way. The law can never bring us into the promised land, but Jesus Christ has brought us in by offering one sacrifice for all times. The New Covenant is a better covenant with better promises because it rests on the faithfulness of our beloved High Priest, Jesus Christ!

## Activations

- Set aside 20-30 minutes for prayer. Ask the Holy Spirit to give you more insight into the High Priestly ministry of Jesus Christ. Write down the revelation and insights you receive.

- Read the two passages from Hebrews that describe the New Covenant (Hebr. 8:10-13, 10:10-18). Read them with the Holy Spirit while inviting Him to highlight some of the truths found within them. Then ask Him for more insight into these truths.

- In this chapter and the previous one, we have looked at Jesus as our King and Priest. We have been made into a royal priesthood. This means that you are a king and a priest. What does this mean? Take some time to study and meditate upon this topic. Ask the Holy Spirit for more revelation and write down your new insights.

- Ask the Holy Spirit to help you walk in your identity as a priest and king. Invite Him to show you what that looks like in your daily life and then start make any of the adjustments that He might show you, to walk in it.

# CHAPTER 19: THE ENCOURAGING LOVE OF JESUS CHRIST

Drinking from the love of Jesus Christ is to drink from an endless source of encouragement and comfort. We will never spend time with Jesus and leave His presence discouraged or disillusioned. Our heavenly Bridegroom is the ultimate encourager and a very good comforter. *"Look at how much encouragement you've found in your relationship with the Anointed One! You are filled to overflowing with his comforting love. You have experienced a deepening friendship with the Holy Spirit and have felt his tender affection and mercy"* (Phil. 2:1 TPT). When Jesus shows up, He always brings an abundance of encouragement and comforting love. A huge part of growing in intimacy with Him, is to learn how to abide in His encouraging love. He wants to cleanse us from all discouragement. One of the ways in which we receive encouragement from Jesus is through prophetic ministry. The prophetic anointing is one of the ways in which Jesus equips us to encourage and comfort one another.

## Love That Strengthens & Encourages

An important part of prophetic ministry is to encourage people to grow and to be built up in Jesus Christ. Prophecy comforts the brokenhearted and strengthens the weak. I often tell people that if you long to grow in the prophetic, a good way to start is by encouraging people. To be an encourager, is to move within the realm of the prophetic. *"But the one who prophesies speaks to people for their strengthening, encouraging and comfort."* (1 Cor. 14:3 NIV). I have found that if a group makes their daily goal to encourage as many people as possible, they will soon start flowing in the gift of prophecy.

Jesus is very passionate for us to fulfill our destiny in God. He will take every opportunity He can to inspire us in our walk with Him. One of the ways that He does this is through prophetic people. Jesus is the blueprint for prophetic ministry, and every prophet is called to reflect His prophetic nature. This is true concerning the prophets in the Bible as well. They serve as a type of Christ. We are now going to look at two of these prophets to learn more about the encouraging love of Christ.

## The Old Testament Prophets

Many of the prophets in the Old Testament would probably have had a hard time fitting into most of our churches. They were wild people, sometimes even a bit extreme. The reason for this is that their lives were meant to be a sign and a wonder to the people of God. God wants to reach the heart of His people and sometimes that involves offending our mind to capture our heart. This is the reason that there is a wild element to the prophetic even in the New Covenant. The prophetic needs to be unbalanced to break through with the message that Jesus is speaking. There is a wild and unpredictable element to the love of Christ. This comes from His burning passion for His bride. But even though this is a part of the nature of the prophetic, all true and authentic prophetic ministry will always be filled with encouragement and comfort. The prophets Haggai and Zechariah are perfect examples of this.

## The Work of Restoring the Temple Starts

Israel had been sent into exile because of their idolatry. Jerusalem with its walls and the temple were left in ruins during this time, but there was still hope. The prophet Jeremiah had prophesied that the people of Israel would return after seventy years in exile (Jer. 25:11-12, 29:10-12). That prophecy was being fulfilled as the first group of exiles returned to Jerusalem. This group was led by

Joshua, the high priest, and Zerubbabel, the governor of Judah. As soon as these exiles returned to Jerusalem, they started to work on restoring the temple. Their work started well, and it all seemed to go according to the plans (Ezra 3:1-13).

## Resistance That Discourages and Hinders the Vision

When the inhabitants of the land, who were enemies of Judah, heard that the temple was being restored, they wanted to join in the work. They were not allowed to do that, since only the people of God could rebuild His temple. Because of this, they started resisting and discouraging the people of Israel in their work (Ezra 4:1-5). The opposition became so fierce that the people of God gave up because of discouragement and fear. *"Then ceased the work of the house of God which is at Jerusalem. So it ceased unto the second year of the reign of Darius king of Persia"* (Ezra 4:23-24). The demonic resistance broke the courage of the leaders, Joshua and Zerubbabel. When leaders lose their courage, the people will lose their vision (Prov. 29:18).

## Broken by Demonic Pressure

Many believers have similar experiences to that of Joshua and Zerubbabel. They had received a vision from God and started to build according to the vision that God had given. These believers knew that they were really doing the will of God and everything started out good. They had a lot of favor from God in their work, which was apparent by the growth of the vision and the miracles that took place. But suddenly, spiritual resistance and opposition started to mount. The battle became very hard and the attacks were so fierce that they gave up. Now they are trapped in a state of pain and condemnation, being stuck in passivity and fear.
We need to know that condemnation never comes from God, because there is no such thing for us who are in Christ (Rom. 8:1).

# The Prophetic Ministry of Haggai and Zechariah

Since Jesus is the ultimate encourager, He will never leave His people in a state of discouragement and confusion. In this case, God raised up two young men, who were probably still in their late teens. They became the prophetic voices that God used to break the yoke of heaviness over Joshua and Zerubbabel.

*When the prophets, Haggai the prophet and Zechariah the son of Iddo, prophesied to the Jews who were in Judah and Jerusalem in the name of the God of Israel, who was over them, then Zerubbabel the son of Shealtiel and Jeshua the son of Jozadak rose up and began to rebuild the house of God which is in Jerusalem; and the prophets of God were with them, supporting them (Ezra 5:1-2 NASB).*

The prophetic preaching of these two young men strengthened the leaders who rekindled their vision and started to rebuild the temple once again. This is the love of Jesus in action. He always comes to lift and inspire His people. The prophets stayed with the leaders, continuing to strengthen and support them. This was needed since Zerubbabel and Joshua needed a continuous flow of encouragement and strength throughout the whole process of rebuilding the temple.

When the bride of Christ becomes passive because we are being weighed down under a burden of heaviness, Jesus is looking for ways to encourage us. He will speak to us directly, but He will also send prophetic voices to renew us. It is important that we learn to receive these people as a gift from God (Matt. 10:41). We all need encouragement at times and Jesus loves to comfort and encourage His bride. I have made it a daily habit to allow Jesus to shower me with His encouragement and affection. I do this by spending time with Him, reading His Word and soaking in His presence. There is a lot of people who need encouragement from

Jesus, so it has become a habit for me to find someone whom I can give prophetic encouragement every day. Looking for ways in which Jesus can speak through me makes life exciting.

## Joshua Was Bound by Accusations

It is fascinating to read the books of Haggai and Zechariah, since they contain the message that God used to encourage Joshua and Zerubbabel in their work of restoration. Jesus showed Zechariah the spiritual realm by opening his eyes to discern what was going on with Joshua there.

*Then he showed me Joshua the high priest standing before the angel of the Lord, and Satan standing at his right to accuse him. And the Lord said to Satan, "The Lord rebuke you, Satan! Indeed, the Lord who has chosen Jerusalem rebuke you! Is this not a log snatched from the fire?" Now Joshua was clothed in filthy garments and was standing before the angel (Zech. 3:1-3 NASB).*

In this vision, Joshua stood before the angel of the Lord. As we have seen earlier, whenever the *"angel of the Lord"* appears in the Old Testament, it is usually speaking about Jesus Himself. This is what is happening here. Joshua is standing before Jesus, and Zechariah sees Satan standing beside Joshua to accuse him. This is the real reason as to why Joshua had become passive. As the pressure of the enemies of Judah grew, so the accusations of the enemy increased as well. Satan was working behind the scenes to steal the vision and anointing of Joshua.

Joshua is dressed in filthy garments, which is a picture of how he had been defiled by guilt and condemnation. He was oppressed because he had come under the accusations of Satan. But this time when Satan opened his mouth, the Lord rebuked him and silenced his accusations.

## Guilt & Condemnation Is Spiritual Defilement

Guilt and condemnation always come from the accuser. When a believer accepts the devil's lies, that person becomes spiritually defiled (Rev. 12:10). Many believers have given up because they have listened to the accusations of Satan. When the believer pays attention to demonic voices, their words can feel more real than the voice of Jesus. I meet many believers who have been trapped by the devil in this way. We need to remember that as we face times of pressure and spiritual resistance, Satan will always use accusation to bind us in guilt and condemnation. He knows that if we listen to him, we will end up in passivity and become harmless to his plans. The good news is that since Jesus cleansed us from all sin and guilt by His blood, there is no longer a valid case to be made against us (Col 2:13-15). In the same way that the Lord rebuked Satan in Zechariah's vision, we can rebuke him in the name of Jesus.

## Joshua Is Cleansed & Restored

There is more encouragement and good news to be found in this vision. Jesus didn't leave Joshua standing in filthy garments. The Lord rebuked Satan and silenced his accusations. This was necessary to clear the spiritual atmosphere and provide spiritual sight, but Joshua still needed to be both delivered and restored.

*And he responded and said to those who were standing before him, saying, "Remove the filthy garments from him." Again he said to him, "See, I have taken your guilt away from you and will clothe you with festive robes." Then I said, "Have them put a clean headband on his head." So they put the clean headband on his head and clothed him with garments, while the angel of the Lord was standing by (Zech. 3:1-5 NASB).*

Jesus told *"those who were standing"* before Joshua to remove his filthy garments. These servants were the angels, the ministering spirits that serve the children of God (Hebr. 1:14). They removed the old filthy clothes of condemnation and shame. Instead, they dressed Joshua in pure new garments, as a sign of how Joshua was being restored back into his identity. He was also restored into functioning as a spiritual leader and high priest. Joshua was now being dressed in the purity and righteousness of Christ and his strength was renewed. Jesus remains at Joshua's side as this is happening. He is personally leading this process of restoration. Jesus doesn't stand at a distance to observe the work of healing and restoration with His people.

When we are weighed down by guilt and condemnation, Jesus deals with the demonic assignments against us, but He doesn't stop there. He cleanses us and restores us by showering us with encouragement and His loving comfort. Jesus sends His angels to minister to us, dressing us in new clothes. He removes our old clothes that have been defiled by accusation and dresses us in His forgiveness and acceptance. Jesus heals and restores from all spiritual defilement and imparts new vision and strength to us.

### Joshua's Calling Is Renewed

Finally, Jesus finishes restoring Joshua by encouraging him to start actively operating in his calling as a high priest and leader. Jesus promises Joshua that when he does that, he will become a leader with governing authority in the house of God. Jesus will also give him free access to the heavenly courts and councils. *"And the angel of the Lord admonished Joshua, saying, "The Lord of armies says this: 'If you walk in My ways and perform My service, then you will both govern My house and be in charge of My courtyards, and I will grant you free access among these who are standing here"* (Zech.

*3:6-7 NASB).* Jesus is never satisfied by just healing and restoring us. He wants to impart His dreams and vision for our future.

When we receive new vision from Jesus, we will find strength to break out of passivity and discouragement. We can then step into the real creativity and freedom of the Spirit. Jesus imparts new and greater visions into our hearts, so that we can live in our full potential as believers, bearing an abundance of fruit that remains (Acts 2:17-21).

### Encouragement and Vision to Zerubbabel

Zerubbabel needed encouragement as well and the Lord used Zechariah to impart new vision and hope to Zerubbabel. He did so by encouraging him to trust in the power of the Spirit and the grace of God to accomplish the restoration of the temple. *"This is the word of the Lord to Zerubbabel, saying, 'Not by might nor by power, but by My Spirit,' says the Lord of armies. 'What are you, you great mountain? Before Zerubbabel you will become a plain; and he will bring out the top stone with shouts of "Grace, grace to it" (Zech 4:6-7 NASB).* Zerubbabel was the political and administrative leader of the returning exiles. That means that he was a practical man, gifted in administration and the area of leadership. His problem was not the spiritual dynamic that had tormented Joshua, the high priest. Zerubbabel's issue was that he trusted in the strength of men to accomplish the work of God. Therefore, he had become tired and discouraged. The Lord's message for him was a simple one, which can be summed up like this: *"My grace is all you need. My power works best in weakness" (2 Cor. 12:9 NLT).*

It is important for us to learn this lesson as well. If we fall into the trap of trusting in human strength to accomplish the work of God, we will quickly get tired and worn out. We live in the New Covenant, which is the covenant and ministry of the Spirit, and it is only by the Spirit of the Lord that we can accomplish the work of Christ (2 Cor. 3:8). We must make the grace of God our only source of strength. When we learn that lesson, all things are possible because the only thing that limits us is the possibilities of God (2 Cor. 3:5-6).

## You Will Fulfill Your Vision

The Lord continued to encourage Zerubbabel by declaring that he would be able to finish the temple. He started the work by restoring the foundation of the temple and God promised to provide the grace to finish the rebuilding of the house of God as well. *"Also the word of the Lord came to me, saying, "The hands of Zerubbabel have laid the foundation of this house, and his hands will finish it. Then you will know that the Lord of armies has sent me to you. For who has shown contempt for the day of small things?" (Zech. 4:8-10 NASB)* God encouraged Zerubbabel not to listen to the people who despised the small beginnings, but to see that with Jesus, small is the new big. The Lord promises that Zerubbabel will rebuild the temple, putting the last stone into place with shouts of *"Grace, grace to it"*!

Jesus encourages us by giving visions and promises that paints a picture of the coming breakthroughs and fulfilled promises on our heart. We should never despise small beginnings because in the Kingdom of God, greatness is often hidden within the plain and unspectacular. *"Heaven's kingdom can be compared to the tiny mustard seed that a man takes and plants in his field. Although the smallest of all the seeds, it eventually grows into the greatest of garden plants, becoming a tree for birds to come and build their nests in its branches" (Matt. 13:31-32 TPT)*. Heavenly dreams and visions are our future in seed form. To keep on listening to the encouraging words of Jesus gives us access to His dreams so that we can see reality through His eyes. The words that Jesus has spoken will always come to pass. Jesus will walk with us through the process of getting there, encouraging us every step of the way (Phil. 1:6)!

## Take Courage!

The book of Haggai is much shorter than that of Zechariah, but it is just as powerful. These books are similar in the sense that they are both words of prophetic encouragement to Zerubbabel, Joshua, and the returning exiles. God promises that if they make the rebuilding of the temple their top priority, His blessings and favor will increase dramatically. The Lord uses the preaching of Haggai to inspire the returning exiles to rise up and continue the work of restoring the temple (Hagg. 1:1-15). Haggai speaks the following word from the Lord to the leaders and all the people who are working:

*Who is left among you who saw this temple in its former glory? And how do you see it now? Does it not seem to you like nothing in comparison? But now take courage, Zerubbabel,' declares the Lord, 'take courage also, Joshua son of Jehozadak, the high priest, and all you people of the land take courage,' declares the Lord, 'and work; for I am with you,' declares the Lord of armies. 'As for the promise which I made you when you came out of Egypt, My Spirit remains in your midst; do not fear (Hagg. 2:1-5 NASB).*

The Lord exhorts both Joshua and Zerubbabel to take courage. Some of the people who had seen the former temple in all its glory, thought that the new and restored version of the temple seemed unimpressive in comparison. They despised the day of small beginnings (Zech. 4:10). But the Lord told them not to listen to that, but to take courage. The Lord Himself was with them and Jesus is always more than enough.

A work that is blessed by the Lord is significant no matter how small it looks in the natural. When we are working on the vision that God has given, there will be negative voices who criticize and put down what we are doing. It is vital that we don't listen to theses voices, but instead keep on listening to the encouraging words of Jesus Christ. Small is always big when the Lord is with us. We must learn to take courage by spending time with Jesus. There we will find the comfort and encouragement to move on with our work and vision.

## Greater Glory Is Coming!

Even if the restored version of the temple seemed small and a bit insignificant in comparison to the old temple of Solomon, God promised that the glory would be greater in the restored temple. Greater glory is more important than a nice appearance.

*For this is what the Lord of armies says: 'Once more in a little while, I am going to shake the heavens and the earth, the sea also and the dry land. I will shake all the nations; and they will come with the wealth of all nations, and I will fill this house with glory,' says the Lord of armies. 'The silver is Mine and the gold is Mine,' declares the Lord of armies. 'The latter glory of this house will be greater than the former,' says the Lord of armies, 'and in this place I will give peace,' declares the Lord of armies (Hagg. 2:6-9 NASB).*

There is nothing more precious than the glory of the Lord. The Lord revealed that the restored temple would become a place of revelation and glory. Because of this, the restored temple would be filled with peace and attract the wealth of the nations. Peace and wealth are always fruits of the manifest glory of the Lord.

We who live in the New Covenant are living in the greater glory. Our vision will be filled with that glory as we remain obedient to the heavenly vision. Jesus is with us and that makes our work significant. Our vision is destined to become a place of peace and wealth, because of the manifest presence of Jesus. Abiding in His love is always the gateway to experience this greater glory. The Holy Spirit ministers to us by glorifying Jesus, and *"…will not the ministry of the Spirit be even more glorious? If the ministry that brought condemnation was glorious, how much more glorious is the ministry that brings righteousness"* (2 Cor. 3:8-9 NIV).

## The Temple Is Finally Restored

The day came when the temple was finally restored. As the work of restoration was coming to an end, we find out how important the prophetic ministry of these two young prophets had really been. They had been strengthening and encouraging the people in a powerful way.

*So the Jewish elders continued their work, and they were greatly encouraged by the preaching of the prophets Haggai and Zechariah son of Iddo. The Temple was finally finished, as had been commanded by the God of Israel and decreed by Cyrus, Darius, and Artaxerxes, the kings of Persia (Ezra 6:14 NLT).*

The ministry of Haggai and Zechariah reveal the encouraging love of Jesus Christ. We should always remember that Jesus is showering us with encouragement and comforting love. And we are invited to abide in His love. As we do that, we will flow in prophetic encouragement, strengthening and building up the bride of Christ in a powerful way.

# Activations

- Set aside 20-30 minutes for prayer. Ask the Holy Spirit to reveal more of the encouraging love of Jesus to you. Invite Jesus to speak encouraging and comforting words to you. Write down what He reveals to you.

- We have studied the prophetic ministries of Haggai and Zechariah as examples of how Jesus encourages us. Find at least two or three other people who flowed in the ministry of encouragement in the Bible. Study their lives and invite the Holy Spirit to give deeper insight into this ministry through them.

- Take some time in prayer to ask the Father to anoint you with prophetic encouragement. Invite the Holy Spirit to guide you in flowing this ministry in a natural way. Make it your daily habit to receive encouragement from heaven and have as a personal goal to encourage at least one person with a word from Jesus every day.

- As you have been doing the activations, you have been made notes on the insights and revelations that you have received from the Holy Spirit. Read through these notes once again and invite Jesus to encourage and comfort you through these notes. Ask Jesus to lead you in finding ways to you can use these revelations to encourage your fellow believers.

# CLOSING WORDS

When I began writing the outline for this book, I had a different book in my mind than the one you have just finished reading. After having written a few chapters, I was preparing to write a chapter on the burning love of Jesus Christ. As I was praying, I found myself being captivated by the beauty and glory of our heavenly Bridegroom. I could not stop beholding Him and this book is the result of that vision. To know that we are united with Him, and that we can live in intimacy with Jesus everyday of our lives, is an amazing honor. You and I have been created to be loved by Jesus and to love Him back forever.

The book that I planned to write were meant to address the pioneering movement of believers who have been raised up through deep encounters with the love of the Father. I'm still planning to write that book, so I guess that will be my next book instead. That seems to be the right order of writing, since every pioneer needs a deep and life changing revelation of Jesus. He is our message, our vision and our life.

To know Jesus and to be transformed into His very image is our destiny. We are in different places on that journey, but before this story is over, Jesus will have the mature bride that He has always longed for. He will personally see to that. *"I pray with great faith for you, because I'm fully convinced that the One who began this gracious work in you will faithfully continue the process of maturing you until the unveiling of our Lord Jesus Christ"* (Phil. 1:6 TPT). I wanted to paint a picture of our beautiful Savior and Bridegroom within these pages. My desire is for all of us to have a greater and deeper vision of who Jesus is.

We are His bride and He loves and favors us deeply. I'll leave you with the final greeting of Paul to the church in Corinth. This is my greeting to you as well:

*Now, may the grace and joyous favor of the Lord Jesus Christ, the unambiguous love of God, and the precious communion that we share in the Holy Spirit be yours continually. Amen (2 Cor. 13:14 TPT).*

# BIBLIOGRAPHY


Unless otherwise indicated, all scriptural quotations are from the *King James Version* of the Bible.

Scripture references marked AMP are taken from Amplified® Bible Copyright © 2015 by The Lockman Foundation, La Habra, CA 90631.

Scripture references marked The Message are taken from The Message. Copyright © 1993, 1994, 1995, 1996, 2000, 2001, 2002.

Scripture references marked NASB are taken from NEW AMERICAN STANDARD BIBLE® NASB® Copyright © 1960, 1971, 1977,1995, 2020 by The Lockman Foundation A Corporation Not for Profit La Habra, CA. All Rights Reserved.

Scripture references marked NIV are taken from the HOLY BIBLE, NEW INTERNATIONAL VERSION®. NIV®. Copyright © 1973, 1978, 1984 by the International Bible Society.

Scripture quotations marked NLT are taken from the Holy Bible, New Living Translation, copyright 1996, 2004, 2007, 2015 by Tyndale House Foundation. Used by permission of Tyndale House Publishers, Inc., Carol Stream, Illinois 60188. All rights reserved.

Scripture references marked NKJV are taken from The Holy Bible, New King James Version, Copyright © 1982 Thomas Nelson. All rights reserved.

# About the Author

Martin Reén lives in the north of Sweden together with His wife Linda, and their children Isak, Benjamin and Noomi. Martin and Linda's vision has always been to know the heart of the Father in deeper ways, to grow in intimacy with Jesus Christ, and to daily be more conformed into His image. They want to introduce as many parts of the body of Christ as possible to the Father's love and the finished work of Jesus Christ, so that believers can be secure in their identity as sons and daughters and live by the life of Christ. Martin and Linda travel all over the world to preach the gospel, and teach in Bible schools, seminars, conferences, and on-line events. They also work with missions, counselling, and leadership training.